Literacy Strategies
for secondary Grades

Laura Keisler, Ed.D.

Contributing Author
Erica Bowers, Ed.D.

Consultant
Jennifer Jump, M.A.

Publishing Credits
Corinne Burton, M.A.Ed., *President* and *Publisher*
Aubrie Nielsen, M.S.Ed., *EVP of Content Development*
Véronique Bos, *Vice President of Creative*
Kyra Ostendorf, M.Ed., *Publisher, professional books*
Cathy Hernandez, *Senior Content Manager*
Fabiola Sepulveda, *Junior Art Director*
Michelle Lee Lagerroos, *Interior Graphic Designer*
David Slayton, *Assistant Editor*

Image Credits
p. 30 Library of Congress; all other images from iStock and/or Shutterstock.

The classroom teacher may reproduce copies of materials in this book for classroom use only. The reproduction of any part for an entire school or school system is strictly prohibited. No part of this publication may be transmitted, stored, or recorded in any form without written permission from the publisher.

Website addresses included in this book are public domain and may be subject to changes or alterations of content after publication of this product. Shell Education does not take responsibility for the future accuracy or relevance and appropriateness of website addresses included in this book. Please contact the company if you come across any inappropriate or inaccurate website addresses, and they will be corrected in product reprints.

All companies, websites, and products mentioned in this book are registered trademarks of their respective owners or developers and are used in this book strictly for editorial purposes. No commercial claim to their use is made by the author(s) or the publisher.

A division of Teacher Created Materials
5482 Argosy Avenue
Huntington Beach, CA 92649
www.tcmpub.com/shell-education
ISBN 978-1-0876-9675-1
© 2024 Shell Educational Publishing, Inc.

Table of Contents

Introduction 1
   What the Science of Reading Says 1
   The Science of Reading: Models of Reading 2
   The Science of Reading: Implications for Teaching 4
   Components of Literacy 7
   Factors That Contribute to Reading and Writing Success 10
   Differentiation 13
   Cultural Relevance 15
   How to Use This Book 17

Section I: Word Recognition and Language Knowledge 19
   Whole-Class Choral Reading (WCCR) 24
   Partner Reading 25
   STRIVE Vocabulary Map 28
   List-Group-Label 32
   Word Nerd 36
   Sort It Out 40
   Word Matrix 44
   DISSECT 48
   Sentence Combining 51
   Grammar Rants 53

Section II: Reading Comprehension and Content Knowledge 58
   Anticipation Guide 65
   Collaborative Concept Map 68
   Text Structure Analysis 70
   Text Analysis Pyramid 79
   Annotation 82
   Annotate and Compare 84
   Structured Annotation 87
   Line-by-Line Reading 89
   GRASP 91
   Thinking at Right Angles 95
   Question Journal 99
   Facts-Questions-Responses (FQR) 103
   Get the GIST 107
   Double Entry Journal 111

Reciprocal Teaching 115
　　Text Rendering 119

Section III: Writing 124
　　Genre Analysis 133
　　EASE (Examine, Assess, Suggest, Envision) 138
　　RAFT 142
　　Expository Writing Frames 145
　　Scholarly Texts 148
　　Planning for Writing 152
　　Composing a Draft 157
　　R.A.C.E. Organizer 162
　　Revising Writing 166
　　Editing Writing 171
　　Reading Response 175
　　Read, Reread, List, Compose (RRLC) 179

References 183
Digital Resources 193

INTRODUCTION

What the Science of Reading Says

This book is one in a series of professional resources that provide teaching strategies aligned with the Science of Reading. The term the *Science of Reading* pervades the national conversation around the best literacy instruction for all students. The purpose of this series is to close the gap between the knowledge and understanding of what students need to become literate humans and the instructional practices in our schools. This gap is widely ackowledged yet remains intact. While research is available, journals are not easy to navigate. However, with concise resources that build understanding of the body of research and offer strategies aligned with that research, teachers can be equipped with the logical steps to find success. This book will help you navigate the important Science of Reading research and implement strategies based on that research in your classroom.

What is meant by the *Science of Reading*? The Science of Reading is the collection of research that leads to the understanding of how students learn to read. Research dedicated to understanding how we learn to read and write has been conducted for more than 50 years. This research has explored topics ranging from the skills needed to read and write, to the parts of the brain involved in reading development, to the best way to teach children how to read. The research clearly demonstrates the following: 1) the most effective early reading instruction includes an explicit, structured, phonics-based approach to word reading; and 2) reading comprehension relies on word reading (being able to decode individual words) and language comprehension (being able to understand what words and sentences mean).

> The Science of Reading is the collection of excellent research that leads to the understanding of how students learn to read.

INTRODUCTION

According to the Report of the National Reading Panel (2000), a comprehensive literacy program should contain explicit skills instruction in phonemic awareness, phonics, fluency, vocabulary, and reading and language comprehension. In addition, effective literacy instruction includes writing instruction. Ideally, this will occur in classrooms that emphasize and facilitate motivation for and engagement in reading through the use of a variety of authentic texts, authentic tasks, cooperative learning, and whole- and small-group instruction that connects reading to students' lived realities. Motivation and engagement are important considerations in our teaching. Cultural and linguistic relevance and responsiveness are essential. Authentic opportunities for speaking, listening, and writing are critical. Gradual release of responsibility is necessary to build independence and is an integral part of promoting a culture of literacy students will embrace and take with them once they leave our care. Let us explore more closely what we can learn from the Science of Reading.

The Science of Reading: Models of Reading

The widely accepted model of the Simple View of Reading (SVR) proposed by Gough and Tunmer (1986) and later refined by Hoover and Gough (1990) depicts reading comprehension as the product of word recognition and language comprehension. This model of reading offers educators a simple, comprehensible way of organizing their understanding of the constructs that can predict successful literacy outcomes (Snow 2018). Hoover and Tunmer (2018) describe these constructs as:

- Word recognition: the ability to recognize printed words accurately and quickly to efficiently gain access to the appropriate word meanings contained in the internal mental lexicon.
- Language comprehension: the ability to extract and construct literal and inferred meaning from speech.
- Reading comprehension: the ability to extract and construct literal and inferred meaning from linguistic discourse represented in print.

Word Recognition (The ability to transform print into spoken language) × **Language Comprehension** (The ability to understand spoken language) = **Reading Comprehension**

The Simple View of Reading

Later work (Hoover and Tunmer 2020; Scarborough 2001) further describes the crucial elements within each of these constructs by incorporating the best of what science tells us about how we read. Scarborough's Reading Rope identifies the underlying skills required for effective and efficient word recognition and language comprehension.

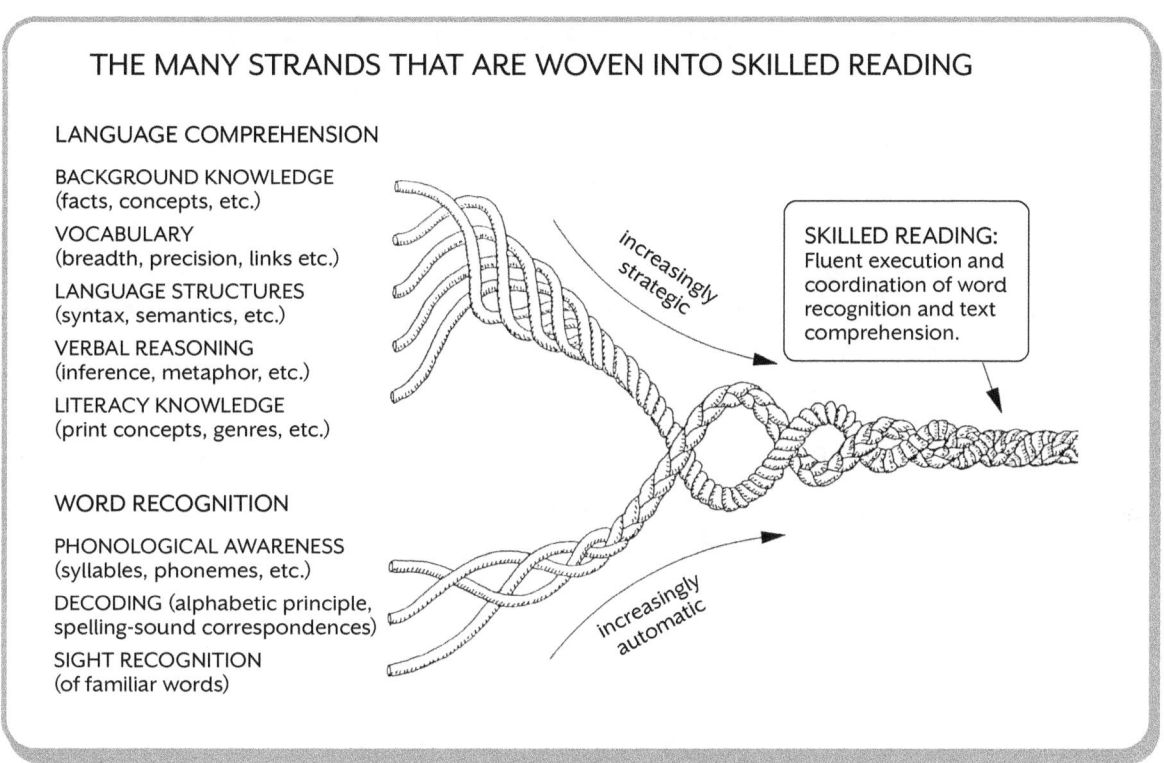

Scarborough's Reading Rope

Credit: Hollis Scarborough, "Connecting Early Language and Literacy to Later Reading (Dis)abilities: Evidence, Theory, and Practice" in *Handbook of Research in Early Literacy*, edited by Susan B. Neuman and David K. Dickinson © Guilford Press, 2001.

Wesley Hoover, William Tunmer, Philip Gough, and Hollis Scarborough are psychologists who dedicated their research to understanding what reading is and what must be present or learned for reading to occur. They have described SVR as simple because it is intended to focus our attention on what is important in reading but NOT to explain the process of *how* reading happens. Similarly, Scarborough expanded on SVR to focus attention on more specific details of language comprehension and word recognition such as prior knowledge and phonological awareness, attempting to include space for process with the addition of automaticity and strategy. Both SVR and the Reading Rope are models—hypotheses that attempt to explain the phenomena of reading. The models describe necessary but not sufficient conditions for reading. Many teachers know that decoding skills can be present, language comprehension can be apparent, and yet comprehension can be impeded. These foundational models do not account for motivation, development, social emotional considerations, linguistic differences, and a host of other factors relevant to literacy teaching and learning.

> INTRODUCTION

In the use and understanding of these models, one can see how the Science of Reading brings together expertise across disciplines. These models of skilled reading provide a roadmap for researchers and classroom educators for the development of instructional practices that promote these essential skills.

The Science of Reading: Implications for Teaching

Here is where we are wise to remember the Science of Reading relies on the *sciences* of reading. It encompasses many fields. The modeling work of cognitive and educational psychologists informs the work of others in literacy research. The work of literacy researchers informs the work of those who translate it into instructional practices. The end goal is to explain the processes by which successful reading occurs and the most effective ways to develop skills that enable these processes. As Louisa Moats declared, *teaching reading is rocket science!* In this seminal piece, Moats describes how teachers can think about the Simple View of Reading in relation to their classroom practice:

> The implications of the Simple View of Reading should be self-evident: reading and language arts instruction must include deliberate, systematic, and explicit teaching of word recognition and must develop students' subject-matter knowledge, vocabulary, sentence comprehension, and familiarity with the language in written texts. Each of these larger skill domains depends on the integrity of its subskills. (Moats 2020, para. 11)

Moats's description reflects the recommendations of the National Reading Panel (NRP) (2000) and the modeling by the cognitive scientists. The evidence base from the sciences that informs our understanding of reading consistently supports systematic and direct instruction in the five components of reading: phonemic awareness, phonics, fluency, vocabulary, and comprehension.

Phonological Awareness and Phonemic Awareness

Phonological awareness is an umbrella term that refers to noticing and manipulating sounds in speech, for instance, individual words, syllables, and sounds in words. *Phonemic awareness*, a subcategory of phonological awareness, is the understanding that spoken words are made of individual sounds called *phonemes*. Research demonstrates that phonemic awareness can be taught and that this teaching is effective for a variety of learners (NRP 2000; National Early Literacy Panel 2008). It assists children in learning to read and learning to spell. Explicitly teaching children to manipulate phonemes, focused on one or two types of phoneme manipulations rather than multiple types, and teaching children in small groups is most effective (National Reading Panel 2000). Phonemic awareness instruction should occur in grades 1 and 2 as needed.

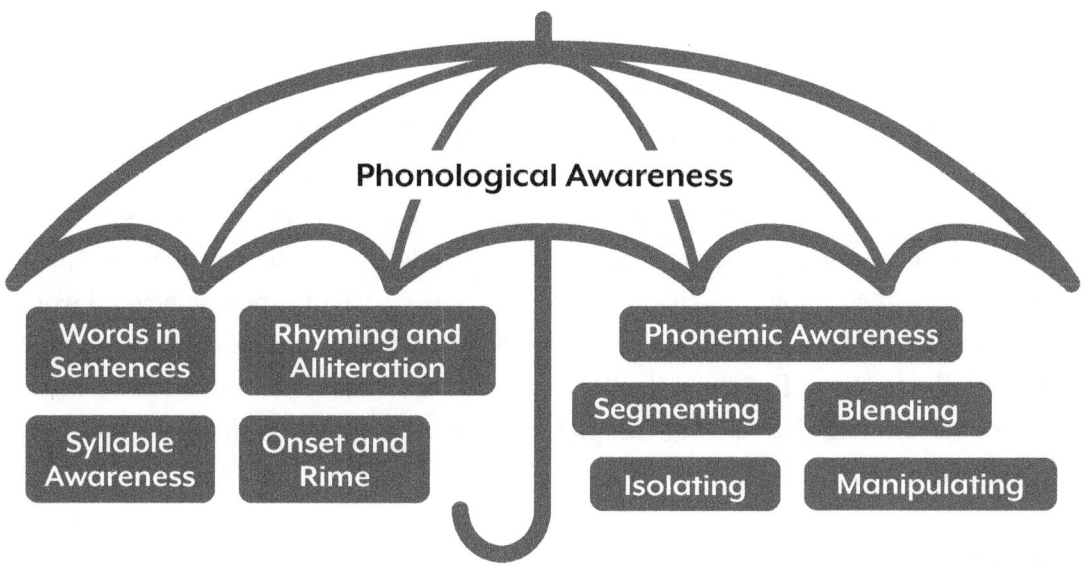

Phonics

Phonics is the term used to describe the relationships between the letters (graphemes) of written language and the individual sounds (phonemes) of spoken language. Phonics instruction helps children learn and use the alphabetic principle—the understanding that there are systematic and predictable relationships between written letters and spoken sounds (Armbruster, Lehr, and Osborn 2010). Children need knowledge of phonics to become efficient, automatic decoders of written text. Explicit, systematic instruction in phonics has been shown to be most effective (National Reading Panel 2000). Three complementary approaches should be used when teaching phonics: (1) *synthetic phonics*, which emphasizes teaching students to convert letters into sounds and then to blend sounds to form words; (2) *analytic phonics*, during which children do not pronounce sounds in isolation but rather learn to analyze letter-sound relationships in previously learned words; (3) *analogy-based phonics*, in which children learn to use parts of word families they know to recognize new unknown words which may contain the same parts. Explicit and systematic instruction in phonics provides students instruction in letter-sound (grapheme-phoneme) connections. This graphophonemic knowledge is essential for decoding mastery. Students must be provided instruction that engages the opportunity to hear, say, read, and spell words both in and out of context. This instruction should happen for students in grades K through 2. Foundational phonics skills instruction for students in intermediate and secondary grades may be provided as interventions to fill gaps in knowledge.

Moving beyond foundational phonics, word study is essential for building students' word recognition skills. The focus is on multisyllabic words and morphology, or the study of words and their parts. Students begin to comprehend the meaning of words by breaking longer words apart. They learn to see how words are connected and build on each other through similarities in their individual parts, such as roots and affixes.

Fluency

Fluency is defined as the ability to read with speed, accuracy, and proper expression. It is a critical component of skilled reading. Fluency depends upon well-developed word recognition skills readers can apply to silent reading or reading aloud that make word reading rapid, accurate, and cognitively efficient. When children are fluent readers, they spend less time trying to decode or pronounce words and can better attend to the comprehension of text. However, fluency also represents a level of expertise beyond word recognition accuracy (National Reading Panel 2000). Phrasing, intonation, and monitoring reading are all considered fluency skills. Research demonstrates that students benefit from fluency instruction and that reading comprehension may be aided by fluency (National Reading Panel 2000).

Vocabulary

Vocabulary refers to the words we must understand to communicate effectively. Vocabulary plays an important role in reading comprehension. Students who develop strong vocabularies and continue to deepen and broaden their vocabulary knowledge find it easier to comprehend more of what they read, especially as text becomes more complex (Sinatra, Zygouris-Coe, and Dasinger 2012). Moreover, students who have strong vocabularies have less difficulty learning unfamiliar words because those words are likely to be related to words that students already know (Rupley, Logan, and Nichols 1999). Researchers and educators often refer to and consider four types of vocabulary: *listening vocabulary* consists of the words we need to know to understand what we hear; *speaking vocabulary* consists of words we use to speak; *reading vocabulary* refers to the words we need to understand what we read; and *writing vocabulary* is the words we use in writing (Armbruster, Lehr, and Osborn 2010). Research reveals that most vocabulary is learned indirectly, but some must be taught directly (Armbruster, Lehr, and Osborn 2010). Vocabulary instruction should be direct and explicit.

> Students who develop strong vocabularies and continue to deepen and broaden their vocabulary knowledge find it easier to comprehend more of what they read.

Comprehension

Research repeatedly demonstrates that students benefit greatly from direct, explicit instruction in reading comprehension strategies and instruction in other areas that support reading comprehension (Duke, Ward, and Pearson 2021; Duke and Pearson 2002; Durkin 1978; Pressley and Afflerbach 1995). The National Reading Panel (2000) identified a number of effective strategies for teaching comprehension. These strategies include vocabulary development, prediction skills (including inferencing), the building of a broad base of topical knowledge, the activation of prior knowledge, think-alouds, visual representations, summarization, and questioning. Students also need to develop their metacognitive skills to become strategic and independent readers. Metacognitive skills, also referred to as *metacognition*, are most simply understood as thinking about one's thinking. This includes skills such as self-questioning, making connections, predicting, and visualizing. Most literacy researchers agree that metacognition plays a significant role in reading comprehension (Baker and Brown 1984; Gourgey 1998; Hacker, Dunlosky, and Graesser 1998; Palinscar and Brown 1984). Research shows that teachers should foster metacognition and comprehension monitoring during comprehension instruction because in doing so, students will be able to monitor and self-regulate their ability to read.

Throughout this book, we delve more deeply into each of these areas to share and explain the research as it applies to specific areas of reading development and to students of different grade levels.

Components of Literacy

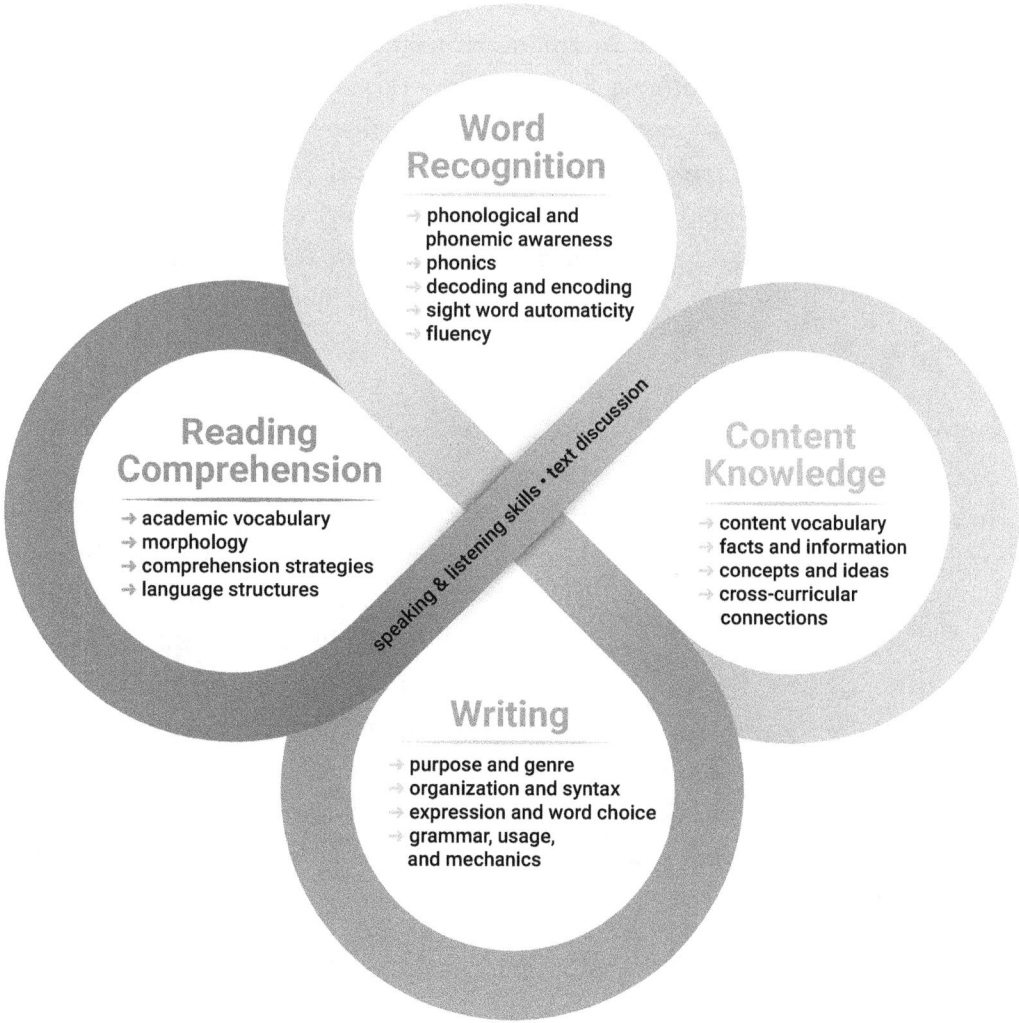

INTRODUCTION

The figure on page 7 reflects what we know to be essential components of comprehensive literacy instruction. This visual representation of the Science of Reading brings together what we know from multiple sciences of reading and literacy, from research in early literacy, from research on the reading writing connection, from the national reports on reading and literacy, and from the cognitive sciences. Development of skills in word recognition, comprehension, content knowledge, and writing are well supported in the research as effective practices for literacy instruction. The figure includes the five components of reading recommended by the National Reading Panel, however the reorganization of these components into the four constructs is quite intentional and represents the evolution in understanding the connections between reading and the wider consideration of what it means to be literate. Just as the SVR was intended to call our attention to the components of reading comprehension (Hoover and Tunmer 2022), the subcategories describing each component of this model give us guidance as to where to focus our teaching in order to support skilled reading and literacy development.

The inclusion of *content knowledge* as a separate construct is important in this model. Research has long struggled over the role of content knowledge in reading comprehension. We are well aware of the fact that the activation and development of prior knowledge (schema) is important to comprehension, we know knowledge of words and word parts play key roles in the decoding of new and/or unfamiliar words and determining the meaning of such words. Of primary importance for activating prior knowledge is the presence of relevant knowledge. There is a growing body of research that demonstrates the critical role of content knowledge in comprehension of text concerning that topic. In fact, the knowledge a reader brings (content and word knowledge) is the primary determinant of comprehension (Anderson and Pearson 1984; Cabell and Hwang 2020). Content knowledge can support readers in making inferences and connections to text. This can deepen understanding of a text and support learning as readers are better able to connect what they read in text to existing schema in ways that develop new learning (Cabell and Hwang 2020). Cabell and Hwang's (2020) recent review of research on content-rich literacy instruction demonstrates its important role in developing language and knowledge in support of reading comprehension. The inclusion of content knowledge as a separate and co-important construct in this model also serves as an important reminder that the Science of Reading goes beyond the narrow discussion of skills-based decoding instruction and that our literacy instruction should be embedded in meaningful context.

> There is a growing body of research that demonstrates the critical role of content knowledge in comprehension of text concerning that topic.

Including *writing* as a component in the model draws attention to the important role writing plays in literacy development and the reciprocal relationship writing shares with reading. Decades of research demonstrate that direct and explicit teaching of writing skills, strategies, and processes are effective at improving students' writing and communication skills (Graham et al. 2012b). There is great benefit to bringing reading and writing study and practice together (Graham 2020). Reading and writing draw from a shared set of literacy knowledge and skills including vocabulary development, background knowledge, and an understanding of syntax, semantics, and morphology. Additionally, reading across genres to understand how one communicates in a particular genre can inform writing in that genre. Writing in response to reading makes comprehension "visible" as students summarize, explain, infer, and make connections to what they have read.

Finally, wrapping the components of this literacy model in a "ribbon" of speaking and listening serves as a powerful reminder that speaking and listening are essential to literacy development. Though reading and writing are not natural processes, our brains are hardwired for communicating through speaking and listening (Hulit, Howard, and Fahey 2018). Researchers and experienced educators can attest to the fact that listening comprehension skills and oral language abilities are generally more developed than students' reading and writing skills, particularly in younger children (Sticht and James 1984). Drawing on the stronger listening comprehension skills of young readers can enhance vocabulary development, grow knowledge of complex language structures, and aid content knowledge as students can comprehend through listening what they would not be able to read. Larger vocabularies and broad content knowledge in turn support reading comprehension and writing skills. As students' reading and writing skills progress, it is important that speaking and listening skills do the same. Speaking is directly connected to our thinking and learning. Opportunities to talk to others about our thoughts require us to be active in our thinking, making decisions about how to explain understanding and reflect and analyze what we know or may not know. These conversations and discussions can help students make sense of new information and construct new meaning (Barnes and Todd 1995; Halliday 1975). Speaking and listening support the development of all other literacy skills, including reading comprehension and writing, and must be an essential element of effective literacy instruction.

> Speaking and listening support the development of all other literacy skills, including reading comprehension and writing, and must be an essential element of effective literacy instruction.

The model promotes literacy instruction that brings together multiple sciences of reading, with the ultimate goal of developing reading, writing, and communication.

INTRODUCTION

Factors That Contribute to Reading and Writing Success

As mentioned above, success in reading and writing can be influenced by more than just explicit instruction in the components of literacy. Duke and Cartwright's (2021) Active View of Reading points to important factors that impact students, including cultural knowledge, motivation and engagement, and executive functioning skills. Each of these can be a determiner of student success. As well as addressing the needs of those students who are progressing at different rates, differentiation is essential for providing all students with the necessary tools for success. Many students enter our classrooms speaking a language other than English and need extra support while attaining English language proficiency. Below is a discussion of how teachers can create a supportive classroom environment and address these additional factors.

Motivating Students to Read

Ensuring that students are interested and engaged in the work of reading is one aspect of instruction that cannot be overlooked. Teachers must identify a range of ways to both engage and motivate their students.

INTERESTS

To foster a lifelong love for reading and writing that extends beyond the day-to-day literacy tasks of classroom life, teachers should become familiar with students' interests as early in the school year as possible with the goal of providing students with reading materials and writing assignments throughout the year that are tailored to their interests, passions, and wonderings. Finding what students are passionate about supports their willingness to engage with text. Ensuring that students have access to a wide range of texts will help each student find something to be passionate about. Providing suggestions rather than rules about the types of texts to read allows for students to choose books that are informational, or contain poetry, or fables, or stories. Once these high-interest texts and assignments are made available, students are more likely to be self-motivated to read and write because they want to discover and share more about the topics that interest them. This self-motivated act of reading and writing develops students' desire to learn that is so important in accessing content from a wide range of texts and text types beyond their interests. Reading and writing about texts of interest allows students to fine-tune their skills in the context of experiences that are interesting, familiar, and comfortable for them, in turn providing them with the confidence and practice needed to effectively navigate texts that are more advanced, unfamiliar, or unexciting.

> Ensuring that students have access to a wide range of texts will help each student find something to be passionate about.

AUTHENTIC OPPORTUNITIES

There are several ways to offer authentic opportunities for students to purposefully engage with interesting texts. Challenge students to use reading to solve a problem, research something of interest, or compare characters they fall in love with. Reading challenges such as these can be formulated and scripted by the teacher, or they can be generic and allow for students to both create the pathway and discover the journey. For example, if a group of students shows interest in the civil rights movement after a social studies lesson, provide a text set for them to engage with. Allow for students to choose which texts to read, which pathway to follow, and how they will share what they have learned. Similarly, if a group of students shows interest in a character, put together a set of texts with similar characters. Provide students with the challenge: discover who is most interesting and prove it. These types of opportunities increase student time spent reading and writing. Without motivation, students will spend less time reading and writing, providing less opportunity to perfect literacy skills, build knowledge, and develop wide vocabulary.

> Teachers who talk enthusiastically about books they have read and who model reading and writing as enjoyable and fulfilling experiences foster a love for reading and writing in their students.

OUTSIDE READING

In addition to discovering students' interests and providing suggestions and texts based on your findings, one of the easiest and most effective ways to improve reading comprehension and writing ability is to promote extensive reading outside of class. Students who frequently read a wide variety of materials have better vocabularies and better reading comprehension skills. They also can use those texts as models for future writing. As Randall Ryder and Michael Graves (2003) point out, wide reading fosters automaticity in students because it exposes them to more words in different contexts, provides them with knowledge on a variety of topics, and promotes lifelong reading habits.

A teacher's attitude toward reading and writing, especially for pleasure outside of school, has a tremendous effect on the students in the classroom. Teachers who talk enthusiastically about books they have read and who model reading and writing as an enjoyable and fulfilling experience foster a love for reading and writing in their students. Teachers who can recommend books that are particularly engaging and interesting to teens can increase student motivation tremendously. Teachers should have an intimate knowledge of reading materials for a wide range of abilities so they can recommend books to any student to read outside of class.

HELPING STUDENTS FIND BOOKS

A powerful step is to help students find sources for books. While many teachers in grades 6 to 12 have classroom libraries, students should have multiple ways to independently access books, both in and out of school.

The school library: Collaborate with the school librarian or media specialist to plan an orientation visit to the school library. During this time, encourage students to explore both informational and fictional books. One way to help students become familiar with the school library is to send them on a library quest. Create a questionnaire that orients students to the different sections of the library and encourages them to find books that capture their interest. Ensure that students have time to visit the library to discover leisure reading materials as well as for research purposes.

The public library: Students will benefit from knowing the location and hours of the local public library. If possible, work with the public librarian to plan a field trip to the library. Students can learn about the different types of media and resources the library offers, as well as the services it provides. A field trip should also include an overview of how to use the library catalog and the steps for obtaining a library card.

Digital libraries: Most public libraries have digital collections that can be accessed anytime and anywhere by library card holders. Depending on the library, these collections include ebooks, audiobooks, comics and graphic novels, magazines, newspapers, and movies. In addition to public libraries, a browser search of "free books for teens" provides a list of websites.

Book clubs: Many libraries have book clubs for teens that meet in person or virtually. Some book clubs focus on specific genres, such as graphic novels. One large, forum-style book club is at **www.goodreads.com/group/show/26225-kids-teens-book-club**. Guides for starting your own book club can also be found online.

TIPS TO PROMOTE READING

- Create a book display of several books in your classroom and refresh the display every few weeks. Give book talks on the books, or have a student who has read a book tell the class about it. Feature books from a range of genres and topics. Connect these books to content students are interested in.

- Remind students that they can abandon books that are not holding their attention. A brief discussion with a student about why they abandoned a book will give you insights into their interests.

- If students are not doing any reading outside of school, provide some time for students to read in class. It may be challenging to block out time for silent reading in today's classrooms, but more reading leads to better reading, faster reading, better writing, more writing, and better language acquisition for English learners (Krashen 2009).

While we can help students find books they are interested in, success may still be hindered if we neglect to address their individual needs. This means meeting students where they are and providing appropriate instruction and support, whether they are English learners, striving readers, or accelerated learners.

Differentiation

As teachers, we know that students come into our classrooms at varying reading, writing, and readiness levels to access the content at hand. This resource provides suggestions for differentiating the strategies for different groups of students so that they can benefit from the strategy being implemented, whether those groups are English learners, striving (below grade level) students, or accelerated (above grade level) students. All students in our classrooms deserve access to rich and rigorous content. Differentiating the content, the process, the product, and the environment allows for all students to find success in learning to read and write.

Our goal is to help students acquire proficiency in reading and writing. As part of this goal, it is our responsibility to provide students with meaningful and interesting contexts to learn language and build their reading and writing skills. In doing so, teachers simultaneously aid in the development of students' collaborative, communicative, and group-based skills emphasized in speaking and listening standards, subsequently helping all students to strategically communicate and interact with those around them within the context of the English language.

> Differentiating the content, the process, the product, and the environment allows for all students to find success in learning to read and write.

English Learners

When implementing the strategies in this book, discuss with students the importance of using a variety of strategies to understand and write about the new information that they glean from text so that the importance of reading and developing fine-tuned reading and writing skills is effectively communicated and made known. The explicit instruction of these reading and writing strategies provides all learners with meaningful contexts for learning language, so this discussion is necessary for establishing a reason for reading and writing, not only for your English language learners, but for all of your students. It is important to note that providing English learners with scaffolds for accessing content, developing literacy skills, and engaging with the context of unfamiliar cultural references that native English speakers are naturally more familiar with builds pathways for all students to find success. Giving English learners access to texts that will help develop their overall reading abilities is also essential to developing their writing skills. Ample opportunities to engage with rich content also support multilingual students in developing the knowledge and vocabulary that underpin their understanding. In addition, English learners "will benefit from actively seeking exposure to language and social interaction with others who can provide meaningful input in the second language. Furthermore, they—and you, the teacher—can enhance students' English language skills by placing language learning in meaningful and interesting contexts" (Dunlap and Weisman 2006, 11).

Striving Learners

In addition to building motivation through interest-based texts, striving students will benefit from scaffolding. While all students benefit from explicit, authentic instruction, these are crucial elements for striving readers. Striving readers can benefit from participating in a small group before the whole-class lesson to have the opportunity to learn the information in a lower-risk environment, with text at a developmentally appropriate level. In addition, they may need additional practice with the content after instruction. It is vital that striving learners are provided with additional scaffolds to ensure their success.

Accelerated Learners

While it is critical to differentiate lessons for striving learners, accelerated students also benefit from modifications to instruction. Teachers can challenge accelerated learners by extending the content either in depth or breadth (Tomlinson 2014). In addition, teachers can provide accelerated learners with opportunities to demonstrate their understanding of content by modifying the process (how students are provided the content) or the product (what students produce to demonstrate understanding). Adapting curriculum for accelerated learners also addresses issues of motivation, as providing tasks that are cognitively challenging maintains their interest.

Throughout this text, we recommend differentiating the lessons to better accommodate all students. Some modalities we recommend are whole class, small groups, collaborative learning, and partner pairs.

Whole class may be used for:

- introducing a new strategy
- modeling think-alouds to show students how to use the strategy
- practicing think-alouds and allowing students to share their experiences and ideas using the strategy

Small groups may be used for:

- pre-teaching new strategies and vocabulary to English learners or striving students
- providing more intensive instruction for striving students

- checking students' understanding of how to apply strategies to the text they are reading or composing
- introducing accelerated students to a strategy so that they can apply it independently to more challenging texts
- encouraging students to use a strategy to think more deeply than they might have imagined possible

Collaborative learning may be used for:

- allowing students to practice strategies without teacher involvement (the teacher is available and "walking the room" to monitor group progress and understanding)
- providing striving students with peer support in completing tasks when groups are strategically formed

Pair students with partners to:

- strategically scaffold and support their learning (e.g., pair a striving student with a "near-peer"—someone who is just ahead of their partner)
- share responses and ideas when trying out strategies

Cultural Relevance

Students learn best when they feel they can take risks and be open to new experiences. For this to happen, teachers need to create a space where everyone feels valued and that they belong. One way to do this is to design a classroom that represents the diverse background and culture of our students. Being mindful of students' home lives, cultures, and language experiences is known as being culturally and linguistically responsive. According to Sharroky Hollie, cultural and linguistic responsiveness (CLR) can be defined as the "validation and affirmation of the home (indigenous) culture and home language for the purposes of building and bridging the student to success in the culture of academia and mainstream society" (2018, 23).

Being a culturally and linguistically responsive educator is a journey. The concepts may be well-known, or they may be new. Culturally and linguistically responsive educators are self-aware and socially aware. They are aware of their own cultural backgrounds, which include ethnicity, nationality, religion, age, and gender, among other things. In the classroom, CLR educators are responsive to cultural differences and have an unconditional positive regard for students and their

> In the classroom, culturally and linguistically responsive educators are sensitive to cultural differences and have an unconditional positive regard for students and their cultures.

INTRODUCTION

cultures. They strive to continually learn about students and their cultures, adjusting their perspectives and practices to best serve students.

Culturally and linguistically responsive classrooms are print-rich and display the linguistic supports multilingual learners and others need to be successful. This includes the academic vocabulary that students are learning, which they need to access to be able to discuss language and content. In addition, CLR classrooms are active. Students utilize the four language domains and are engaged in discussions with peers and teachers. They are physically active and move around the room to work with peers on a variety of projects. The materials being utilized reflect a variety of cultures and perspectives, and student work is prominently displayed and honored.

> Culturally and linguistically responsive educators design curriculum by selecting texts with characters and pictures that represent their students.

Culturally and linguistically responsive educators design curriculum by selecting texts with characters and pictures that represent their students. They create shared writing pieces that draw from the students' home languages and cultures. They encourage students to research areas of interest and produce art that validates and exhibits their culture. Culturally and linguistically responsive educators are constantly re-evaluating their curricular choices to ensure all students are represented and validated.

Hollie (2018) embraces a philosophy of affirming students' home cultures and languages and suggests educators "love outrageously." To be culturally and linguistically responsive, educators must know their students. When educators validate students' cultures and languages through classroom management and materials, they help students see themselves reflected in the curriculum and allow students to use their backgrounds to supplement the classroom learning environment.

Taking a culturally and linguistically responsive stance is a holistic approach. It embraces the whole learner. When students feel they belong, are validated, and are represented in the curriculum, they are open and connected to the learning. Teaching in this manner allows for everyone's story to be told.

How to Use This Book

This book includes a variety of strategies that can be integrated into any language arts curriculum to improve students' reading and writing skills: promoting word consciousness, analyzing word parts, activating and developing knowledge through vocabulary development and content learning, using think-alouds and monitoring comprehension, questioning, summarizing, using visual representations and mental imagery, using text structure and text features, incorporating mentor text, using graphic organizers, and modeling writing. These research-based instructional strategies will help teachers bridge the gap between the science of literacy instruction and classroom practice.

The strategies are presented in three sections: I) Word Recognition; II) Reading Comprehension and Content Knowledge; and III) Writing. The strategies in these sections correspond with key competencies identified in the What the Science of Reading Says series (Jump and Johnson 2023; Jump and Kopp, 2023; Jump and Wolfe 2023).

Each section opens with an overview of research in that area to emphasize the importance of that particular component. There is also a clear and detailed explanation of the component, suggestions for instruction, and best practices. This information provides teachers with the solid foundation of knowledge to provide deeper, more meaningful instruction to their students.

Following each overview are a variety of instructional strategies to improve students' reading and writing. Each strategy in the book includes

- background information that includes a description and purpose of the strategy, and the research basis for the strategy
- the objective of the strategy
- a detailed description of how to implement the strategy, including any special preparation that might be needed
- suggestions for differentiating instruction

When applicable, the strategy includes one or more activity sheets as reproducibles in this book and in the digital resources. Grade-level examples of how the strategy is applied are also included when applicable. For more information about the digital resources, see page 193.

SECTION I:
Word Recognition and Language Knowledge

The strategies in this section correspond with key competencies identified in the What the Science of Reading Says series (Jump and Johnson 2023; Jump and Kopp, 2023; Jump and Wolfe 2023). These research-based instructional strategies will help teachers bridge the gap between the science of literacy instruction and classroom practice.

Strategy	Skills and Understandings Addressed			
	Fluency	Vocabulary Knowledge	Morphology	Syntax and Semantics
Whole-Class Choral Reading	■			
Partner Reading	■			
STRIVE Vocabulary Map		■		
List-Group-Label		■		
Word Nerd		■		
Sort It Out			■	
Word Matrix			■	
DISSECT			■	
Sentence Combining				■
Grammar Rants				■

Word Recognition and Language Knowledge

As students leave elementary school behind and become early adolescent readers, the purposes for and demands of reading change significantly. In grades 6–12, students journey to becoming fully independent readers, a necessary skill for academic success beyond the secondary years and for full participation in professional and civic life as a contributing member of any society. Independent readers are fully capable of comprehending a wide variety of text and media, for enjoyment, for information, and for lifelong learning. Comprehensive literacy development and support through the secondary grades requires continued systematic and explicit instruction in learning to read and comprehend.

> It is imperative that teachers of adolescent readers continue to provide instruction and support in the skills that aid comprehension, such as fluency, word analysis, and vocabulary skills.

Comprehension is ultimately a process rather than a product, and this process requires application of and proficiency in a variety of skills. The skills necessary for comprehension (decoding, fluency, vocabulary, content knowledge) continue to develop during the secondary grades. Gaps in these skills can impede comprehension of grade-level text and the continued development of literacy skills and content knowledge. For this reason, it is imperative that teachers of adolescent readers continue to provide instruction and support in the skills that aid comprehension, such as fluency, word analysis, and vocabulary skills.

Fluency

Reading fluency consists of three components: word identification accuracy, pacing, and prosody. As readers become increasingly strategic and increasingly automatic in their decoding, reading becomes more fluent (Scarborough 2001). When fluent readers read aloud, their reading is accurate, at a quick but natural pace, and has expression. When fluent readers read silently, reading is highly automatic, with readers grouping words together for meaning rather than reading word by word. In the early grades, instruction that builds decoding skills and automaticity supports fluency. Additional explicit instruction and practice in pace, proper expression, vocabulary, and language structures aid the development of fluent readers. In general, fluency should approximate the pace of conversation, about 150 to 200 words per minute for skilled readers (Rayner et al. 2012). When students leave elementary school with poor fluency skills, these issues tend to persist through middle and high school (Paige et al. 2014). Poorly developed fluency skills are a significant factor in explaining achievement disparities among middle and high school students (Paige 2011; Rasinski and Padak 2005). There are several strategies that middle and high school teachers can use in their classrooms to encourage and develop fluent reading in students, including wide reading, increasing reading volume, modeling of fluent reading, and repeated and assisted reading (Rasinski et al. 2017).

Vocabulary Knowledge

As adolescent readers' word knowledge continues to develop, their vocabularies grow ever larger and the quality of knowledge of individual words improves over time, contributing to greater comprehension of what they are reading by freeing up valuable cognitive resources once devoted to recognizing words and uncovering word meanings (Perfetti 1995, 1998; Perfetti et al. 2007; Perfetti and Stafura 2013). An abundance of research has demonstrated the critical role of vocabulary knowledge in reading comprehension (Cromley and Azevedo 2007; Perfetti and Stafura 2013). So much so that researchers have referred to vocabulary knowledge as the "central connection point" between a reader's word recognition knowledge and their comprehension of text (Perfetti and Stafura 2013, 24). Much of the research on vocabulary instruction reviewed by the National Reading Panel was from work with students above third grade, making the recommendations particularly appropriate for adolescent readers (Lee and Spratley 2010). As mentioned previously, the complexity of words students must be able to both decode and comprehend dramatically increases in grades 6–12. The meanings of many of these words hold the key to understanding the information and ideas expressed by authors and to developing content knowledge.

A goal for adolescent readers is the development of increasingly sophisticated and robust academic vocabularies. Academic language refers to the specialized use of language in disciplinary texts (Beck, McKeown, and Kucan 2002). Academic vocabulary has two components: (1) domain-specific academic vocabulary, and (2) general academic vocabulary. Domain-specific academic vocabulary is what most of us likely consider academic vocabulary; these are low-frequency words, mostly confined to use in a specific discipline like math, or science, or history (Baumann and Graves 2010). Teachers may be familiar with the terms "tier 3 words" (Beck, McKeown, and Kucan 2002) or "technical vocabulary" (Fisher and Frey 2008) to describe domain-specific academic vocabulary. Examples include words such as *acronym*, *isosceles*, or *osmosis*. This is the vocabulary one needs

> Developing a robust oral and written vocabulary and the skills to tackle unknown words will accelerate comprehension as students encounter increasingly complex academic and literary texts (Kamil et al. 2008).

to learn conceptual ideas and subject matter information. General academic vocabulary are words that are used across disciplines to explain, describe, and connect ideas and thoughts. These words are what many might consider markers of a sophisticated vocabulary or the language of school, sometimes referred to as "tier 2 words" (Beck, McKeown, and Kucan

2002). *Recognize*, *support*, and *include* are examples of tier 2 words. These more frequently occurring words are often parts of larger word families (*support, supported, unsupportive*), therefore derivational and morphological knowledge are important skills for readers to acquire. An effective academic vocabulary is deep with respect to knowledge of words and word parts. Readers don't necessarily need to know the definitions of an immense number of words but rather must cultivate an understanding of how words relate to concepts, how they relate to one another, and how they may differ across contexts.

Vocabulary development is a vital part of comprehension instruction in grades 6–12. Suggested instruction includes (1) explicit vocabulary instruction focused on definitions and morphological analysis; (2) repeated exposures to new words; (3) multiple exposures to new words through authentic activities like speaking, listening, reading, and writing; and (4) learning strategies to determine the meaning of unknown words independently. Developing a robust oral and written vocabulary and the skills to tackle unknown words will accelerate comprehension as students encounter increasingly complex academic and literary texts (Kamil et al. 2008). The importance of continued development of vocabulary and word knowledge applies to spelling and writing as well. When writers efficiently spell (encode) individual words, they keep track of the topic, organize their thoughts more effectively, and broaden their word choices, leading to better writing (Singer and Bashir 2004).

Knowledge of Syntax and Semantics

An understanding of how language structure works, through the development of syntactical and semantic knowledge, aids reading comprehension. Syntax is the system of how words are arranged to make sense in a language. Syntactical knowledge includes an understanding of the functions of words and the rules of grammar that govern word arrangement, impacting and conveying meaning in a sentence. Semantics refers to the overall meaning of a sentence or the message the words convey. An essential part of semantic knowledge involves knowing how to determine the differences between words that convey similar meanings and understanding how these differences impact meaning, for example, understanding how the use of the word *jog* as opposed to *run* changes the meaning of the sentence. This understanding of the structure of language helps readers process and understand text at the sentence level. While vocabulary development facilitates the understanding of individual words, knowledge of language structure helps readers understand how the arrangement of words in a sentence influences the meaning. Instructional activities that focus students' attention on the sentence level,

> While vocabulary development facilitates the understanding of individual words, knowledge of language structure helps readers understand how the arrangement of words in a sentence influences the meaning.

attending to the ways words, clauses, and phrases combine to make meaning, and building an understanding of figurative language, are effective in developing knowledge of language structure (LeVasseur, Macaruso, and Shankweiler 2008).

Concluding Thoughts

As readers progress through the middle and high school grades, they encounter increasingly complex text and a wide variety of text genres and topics across multiple content areas. Most students begin middle school with a base in word recognition and word knowledge that allows them to read more independently, but as reading volume increases and text becomes more complex, continued skill development is of critical importance. The texts they encounter will require the learning of vocabulary and new syntax, and they will need advanced skills in fluency, comprehension, and the application of prior content knowledge to achieve academic success.

WORD RECOGNITION AND LANGUAGE KNOWLEDGE: FLUENCY

Whole-Class Choral Reading (WCCR)

Objectives
- Read and comprehend complex literary and informational texts independently and proficiently.

Background Information
Whole-Class Choral Reading (WCCR) is an effective and efficient fluency building strategy (Paige 2011). All students are reading at the same time, in unison with the teacher, engaging fluent readers and providing those who struggle with practice with grade-level text (Paige and Magpuri-Lavell 2014). This strategy is best used with textbooks or novels, which may be slightly above some students' reading levels, giving them support in navigating complex text. WCCR gives students an opportunity to practice and improve their fluency without the pressure of reading aloud individually in front of the class (Paige and Magpuri-Lavell 2014).

Materials
- text selection from the curriculum

Process
1. Choose a text, or a section of text, that can be read in about 2 minutes at a typical target rate of about 150 words per minute. This is a conversational fluency rate. Provide each student a copy of the text.
2. Preview the text with students by reading a sentence or two, and review any vocabulary words that may be challenging.
3. Read the text aloud to the class and direct students to follow along. Be sure to model proper pronunciation and phrasing as you read.
4. Invite the class to read the passage aloud in unison. Challenge the class to try and read together, with one voice. This may require starting over once or twice. Walk around the room while the class is reading to monitor individual voices. Provide any coaching or corrective feedback to the class as a group.

Differentiation
WCCR can be used with smaller groups of students who need additional support or to offer challenge text to advanced readers. Research suggests students may benefit from "reading ahead" of the curriculum (Paige and Magpuri-Lavell 2014). Choose texts on topics that students will be learning about during the next week in the curriculum. This builds content knowledge and exposes students to important vocabulary prior to content learning.

WORD RECOGNITION AND LANGUAGE KNOWLEDGE: FLUENCY

Partner Reading

Objectives

- Read and comprehend complex literary and informational texts independently and proficiently.

Background Information

With Partner Reading, students read and reread text with partners. Research demonstrates that Partner Reading improves accuracy in reading and improves comprehension for both readers (Topping et al. 2012). It is associated with positive outcomes for a wide variety of students across all grade levels and is easy to implement across content areas (Fuchs et al. 2001; Rafdal et al. 2011). First, the more fluent reader takes on the role of Reader while their partner is the Listener, providing a model of fluent reading and allowing the Listener to rehearse the text and hear difficult words pronounced. The students switch roles, and the Listener then becomes the Reader and reads the same passage. Students briefly discuss what they just read. Students repeat the steps until the text is complete. Partner Reading can become a routine in any middle or high school classroom.

Materials

- *Partner Reading* (page 27)
- text selection

Process

1. Pair students based on their reading fluency. One student should be a slightly more skilled or fluent reader. The text students will read should be appropriate for both partners. You may wish to consider students' personalities in the pairings as well. With middle and high school students, it is wise to rotate partner assignments when using this routine to help keep students motivated and engaged.

2. Distribute the *Partner Reading* activity sheets. Assign the more fluent reader the role of Reader and their partner the role of Listener for round 1. The Reader reads the selected passage of text aloud while their partner listens. The Listener can make note of any errors in the reading such as mispronunciation or skipped words. After the Reader has finished reading, the Listener provides feedback or asks questions.

3. Partners switch roles, and the Listener now becomes the Reader and reads the same passage aloud. The other partner takes on the role of Listener, following along and noting any errors. Feedback is shared once the Reader has finished the passage.

4. After reading, students discuss what they read by responding to a generic comprehension question such as "What is the main idea of this section?" or "What was this section mostly about?" Or they simply provide a succinct retelling of the text. You may wish to have students record notes of their discussion on the activity sheet.

5. While students are reading, circulate to listen in on the oral reading and comprehension discussions.

6. Students switch roles again and repeat the process with the next passage in the text. The process is repeated until the reading is complete.

7. Allow students time to write a brief summary of the text on the activity sheet.

Differentiation

Accommodate the varying needs of students by differentiating the texts they are assigned to read. Keep in mind, however, that both students in each pair should read the same text.

Name: _____ Date: _____

Partner Reading

Directions: Takes notes about the text. When you and your partner finish reading the entire text, write a summary of what you read.

My Notes

Section # _____

Section # _____

Section # _____

Summary:

© Shell Education

Literacy Strategies—131699

27

WORD RECOGNITION AND LANGUAGE KNOWLEDGE: VOCABULARY

STRIVE Vocabulary Map

Objectives

- Determine or clarify the meaning of unknown and multiple-meaning words or phrases based on grade-level reading and content, choosing flexibly from a range of strategies.

Background Information

The STRIVE Vocabulary Map (Swanson, Vaughn, and Wexler 2017) is a component of Strategies for Reading Information and Vocabulary Effectively (STRIVE), a model for content instruction. Implementation of the model, including the vocabulary map, is quite effective in improving students' content knowledge, vocabulary, and comprehension. The map is used as part of explicit vocabulary instruction before reading and again after reading, providing students with multiple exposures to key vocabulary. Distributed practice through multiple exposures to critical target words deepens word knowledge and builds content knowledge. The vocabulary map provides student-friendly definitions, visual representations, and examples of the word in varying contexts; attends to a word's morphology; provides practice with word associations; and allows students to create their own examples and discuss their understandings with peers.

Materials

- *STRIVE Vocabulary Map* (page 31)
- text selection

Process

1. Prepare for the lesson by choosing one or two words to teach explicitly. These should be words central to understanding the text selection or concept you will be teaching. Prioritize academic words likely to be encountered across a variety of texts and content areas but unlikely to be part of students' general vocabularies or easily learned independently.

2. Create a *STRIVE Vocabulary Map* using the template (page 31). Prepare sections 1, 2, 3, 4, and 5 for students. Develop one or two discussion prompts for the Turn and Talk section.

3. Allow 10 to 15 minutes for this vocabulary work prior to reading or other instruction. Explain to students they will study words central to concepts they will be reading or learning about. Provide each student with a copy of the *STRIVE Vocabulary Map*.

4. Review sections 1 and 2, reading the definition of the word. Direct students' attention to the image in section 3 and explain how it relates to the definition. Turn students' attention back to section 2 and have them underline key words in the definition. Have students share their thoughts about which words to underline.

5. Have students read the sentences in section 4 and decide which sentence uses the word according to the definition that was discussed. Allow students a few moments to share with partners or the whole class.

6. Put the *STRIVE Vocabulary Maps* aside and have students engage in reading and the rest of the lesson. If time is short, save the after-reading vocabulary work for the following day.

7. Review section 5 with students. Explain that based on their reading they should identify the words that are related to the definition of the target word. Have students choose the related words and explain or defend their choices to partners or small groups. Debrief as a class, clarifying as needed.

8. Have students write their own sentences in section 6 using the target word. Prompt them to review the definition and the illustration for support. Have students share their sentences with partners.

9. Direct students' attention to section 7. Think aloud as you analyze the target word morphologically, identifying affixes and removing them to reveal the base. Have students write the base in section 7. Provide students time to generate two or three words that use the same base and write them in section 7. Discuss students' words as a class. If students need support with morphological analysis, work together as a class to generate a short list of new words.

10. Finish by providing students with time to discuss the words using the Turn and Talk prompts.

Differentiation

Unlike many vocabulary activities, STRIVE should not be differentiated by the number or difficulty of target words. The goal of STRIVE is to help build conceptual knowledge, and the word(s) are chosen specifically for this purpose. Provide additional support as needed as students work through each section. Students can work on STRIVE in small groups if necessary. Teachers of older adolescent readers may wish to have students generate their own student-friendly definitions based on class discussions, eventually finding their own visuals, generating example and non-example sentences, and so on. However, the map should always be used to provide explicit instruction of the most important words and should not be used as an entirely independent activity.

STRIVE Vocabulary Map Example

2. Definition

The rebuilding of the South after the Civil War

3. Illustration

4. Context

Circle the correct sentence.

A. My neighbor's house is under reconstruction after a fire.

B. (Formerly enslaved people were given new rights under Reconstruction.)

1. Word: Reconstruction

5. Word Associations

Choose two related words.

A. (restore)

B. freed

C. blemish

D. (unified)

6. Example

Write a sentence or definition that uses the word.

During Reconstruction, Congress passed laws to protect the rights of Black people.

7. Word Building

Write the base and words with the same base.

construct

reconstructed

unconstructed

deconstruct

Turn and Talk

How would you describe the goals of Reconstruction?

Do you believe Reconstruction was a success or failure?

Name: _____ Date: _____

STRIVE Vocabulary Map

Directions: Record a key word related to a text and write about the word and its meaning.

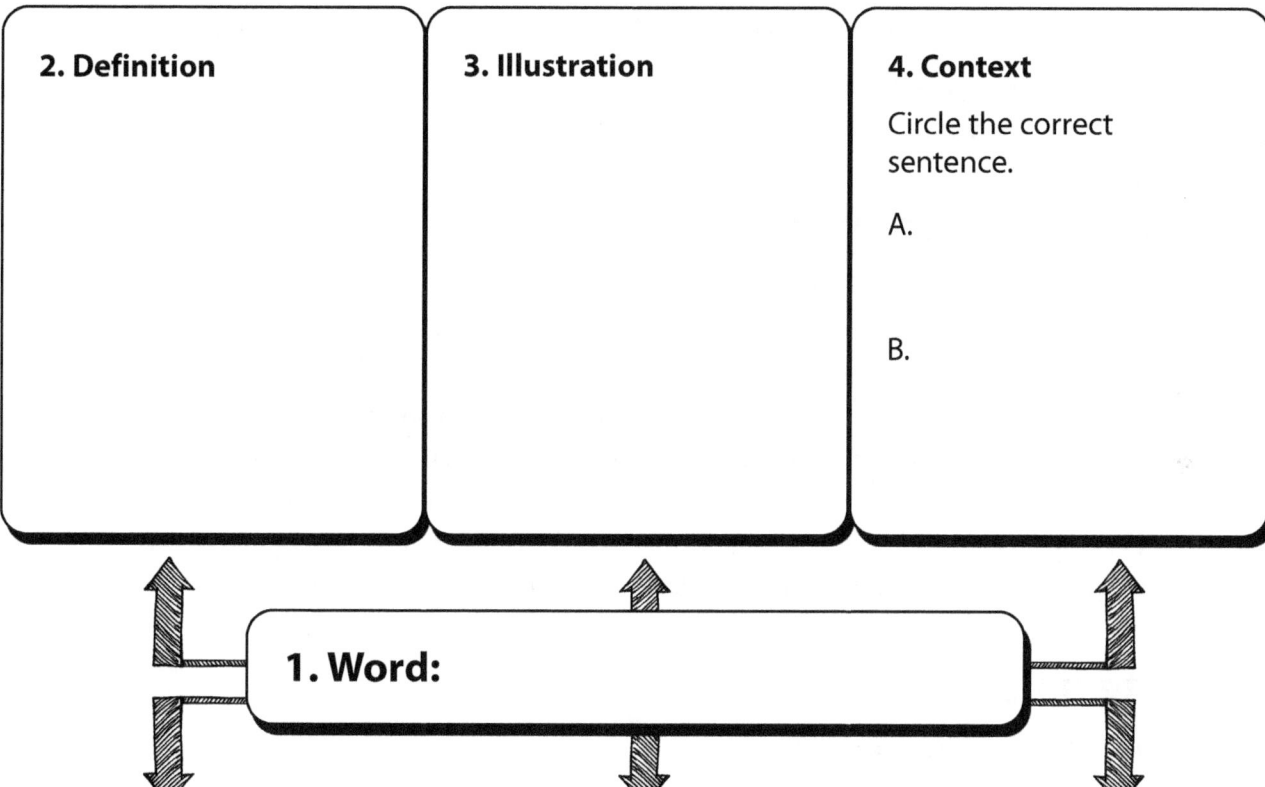

2. Definition

3. Illustration

4. Context

Circle the correct sentence.

A.

B.

1. Word:

5. Word Associations

Choose two related words.

A.

B.

C.

D.

6. Example

Write a sentence or definition that uses the word.

7. Word Building

Write the base and words with the same base.

Turn and Talk

© Shell Education — Literacy Strategies—131699 — 31

WORD RECOGNITION AND LANGUAGE KNOWLEDGE: VOCABULARY

List-Group-Label

Objectives

- Demonstrate understanding of word relationships and nuances in word meanings.
- Acquire and use accurately general academic and domain-specific words and phrases.
- Demonstrate independence in gathering vocabulary knowledge when considering a word or phrase important to comprehension.

Background Information

List-Group-Label (Taba 1967) is a tried-and-true vocabulary strategy that supports academic vocabulary development through semantic mapping. The three-step process engages students in learning new vocabulary and builds categorizing and labeling skills. List-Group-Label activates students' critical thinking skills as they work with classmates to sort and organize content vocabulary. Students use their prior knowledge to discuss words, making decisions about how the words are related to one another and to concepts being studied. List-Group-Label is frequently used before reading or instruction to activate and build prior knowledge, but it can also be used after reading to review vocabulary and concept knowledge.

Materials

- *List-Group-Label* (page 35)
- text selection

Process

1. Prepare by previewing the text students will read. Identify the main concept or topic in the text. This will provide an anchor for students as they generate their lists of words.

2. Introduce the concept or topic and have students brainstorm all of the words they can think of that relate to the concept. Write the words on the board or on chart paper. Expect words that do not relate directly to the concept, and include them on the list. Students will have the opportunity later to discard words they cannot organize into related categories. After students become familiar with this activity, they may work together in small groups to generate the word list.

3. Place students in small groups and provide each student with a *List-Group-Label* activity sheet. Have students work together to organize the list of words by grouping them together into smaller subcategories. Explain to students that as they group

words, they should be able to explain and provide evidence for the subcategories they have created. Students may also provide evidence for discarding words that do not fit into the groups.

4. Ask students to label each of the subcategories. The label should reflect the relationships or connections between the words in a subcategory.

5. Have groups join with another group or come together as a whole class to share and compare their List-Group-Label. This provides an opportunity to further discuss words and potentially reveal additional relationships students didn't identify.

6. Have students read the text selection. Tell them they may modify the List-Group-Label designations as they read if they wish.

Differentiation

List-Group-Label can be done as a whole class, in small groups, in partners, or even individually. To scaffold the activity, preview the reading and generate the list of words for students. Display the lists and have students complete the grouping and labeling steps. Alternately, write the words on sheets of paper, cut them apart, and place them into envelopes. Each group uses the words in the envelope and physically places the words in groups before writing them on the activity sheet.

List Group Label Example

Topic
Climate Change

Word List

greenhouse effect	methane	sea rise
carbon dioxide	trees	UV rays
melting	recycle	volcano
fossil fuel	coal	carbon tax
	permafrost	polar bears
	glaciers	wildfires

Label	Label	Label	Label
Effects	Causes	Possible Solutions	Discarded Words
Group	**Group**	**Group**	**Group**
sea rise	fossil fuel	recycle	polar bears
permafrost	carbon dioxide	carbon tax	
glaciers	volcano	trees	
melting	coal		
wildfires			
greenhouse effect			

Name: _____ Date:_____

List Group Label

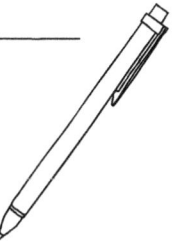

Directions: Group the words into subcategories. Label each group of words.

Topic

Word List

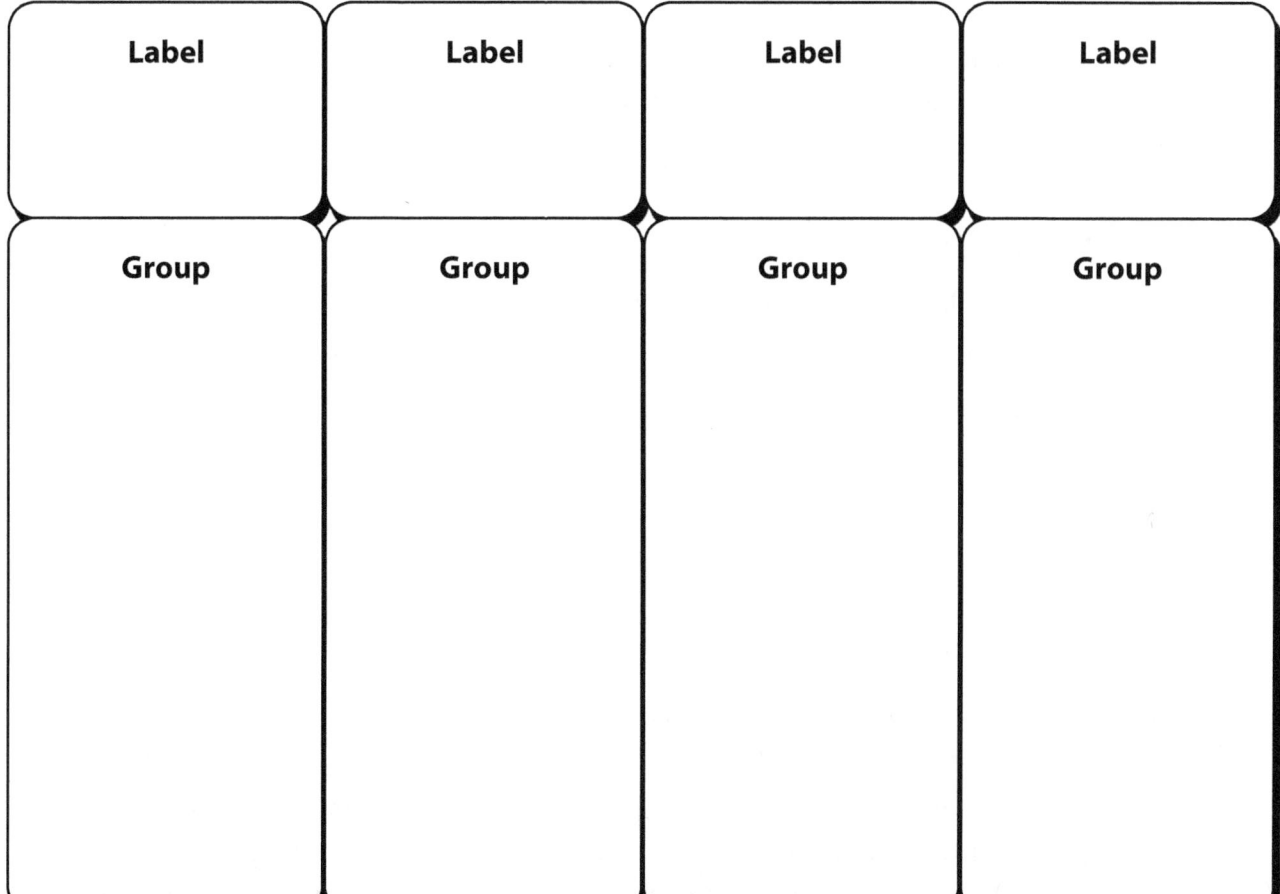

| Label | Label | Label | Label |
| Group | Group | Group | Group |

WORD RECOGNITION AND LANGUAGE KNOWLEDGE: VOCABULARY

Word Nerd

Objectives

- Acquire and accurately use general academic and domain-specific words and phrases.
- Demonstrate independence in gathering vocabulary knowledge when considering a word or phrase important to comprehension or expression.

Background Information

Word Nerd is a strategy for developing independent word learning and word consciousness in older readers. Developing word consciousness involves (1) recognizing semantic relationships between words, (2) understanding that some words have multiple meanings, and (3) noticing when and how new words are used (Watts-Taffe, Gwinn, and Forrest 2018). With Word Nerd, students create personal word journals by recording interesting words that catch their attention while reading, viewing, or listening. Students can record words they are unfamiliar with, words they find interesting, and words taught in class or otherwise selected by the teacher. Research suggests that keeping word journals is a highly effective strategy for developing deeper vocabulary knowledge (McCrostie 2007; Walters and Bozkurt 2009). Devoting one page in the Word Nerd journal to each word, students practice defining words in context, using reference sources to look up definitions, and connecting words to other known words and concepts. These ongoing word journals can be used as a reference during writing and other response activities.

Materials

- spiral notebook or composition book, one for each student
- *Word Nerd* (page 39)
- text selection

Process

1. Prepare for the introductory lesson by selecting a short paragraph from a grade-level text that contains one or more words that would be good candidates for selection into the Word Nerd journal.
2. Introduce the Word Nerd journal by providing each student with a spiral notebook. Explain the purpose of the journal to students.
3. Model how to use the journal by reading aloud the selected passage, thinking aloud as you come across the word you have selected for the demonstration. Display a copy of the *Word Nerd* activity sheet and model how to complete the sheet. Elicit information about related words and definitions in context from students.

4. Distribute copies of the *Word Nerd* activity sheet. Direct students to read a short passage in a textbook or other class reading material and select words to use to practice. Have students complete the *Word Nerd* activity sheets using the words they select.

5. Have students share their selection and completed page with partners.

6. Provide students with clean copies of the *Word Nerd* activity sheet to tape in the front of their journals as a guide. They can add new words directly to the journal pages. Make Word Nerd journals a regular part of the classroom reading routine. Encourage students to record at least one word each time the class reads, and allow time at the end of the lesson or class period for this, or assign it as an independent homework activity. Teachers may wish to incorporate time in the week for students to share with peers the words they have included in their journals that week.

7. In addition to having students record words in their journals, create a class "Word Nerd Word Wall" that students can contribute to as they find new or interesting words in their reading.

Differentiation

While the Word Nerd journal activity is still new, teachers may scaffold the process of learning to keep a word journal by providing students with a few pre-selected words each week and having students add the words to separate pages in their journals. Students then complete all or some of the information for each word independently. Encourage advanced readers to make connections between the words they record and other words they may know such as words that share the same base/root.

Word Nerd Example

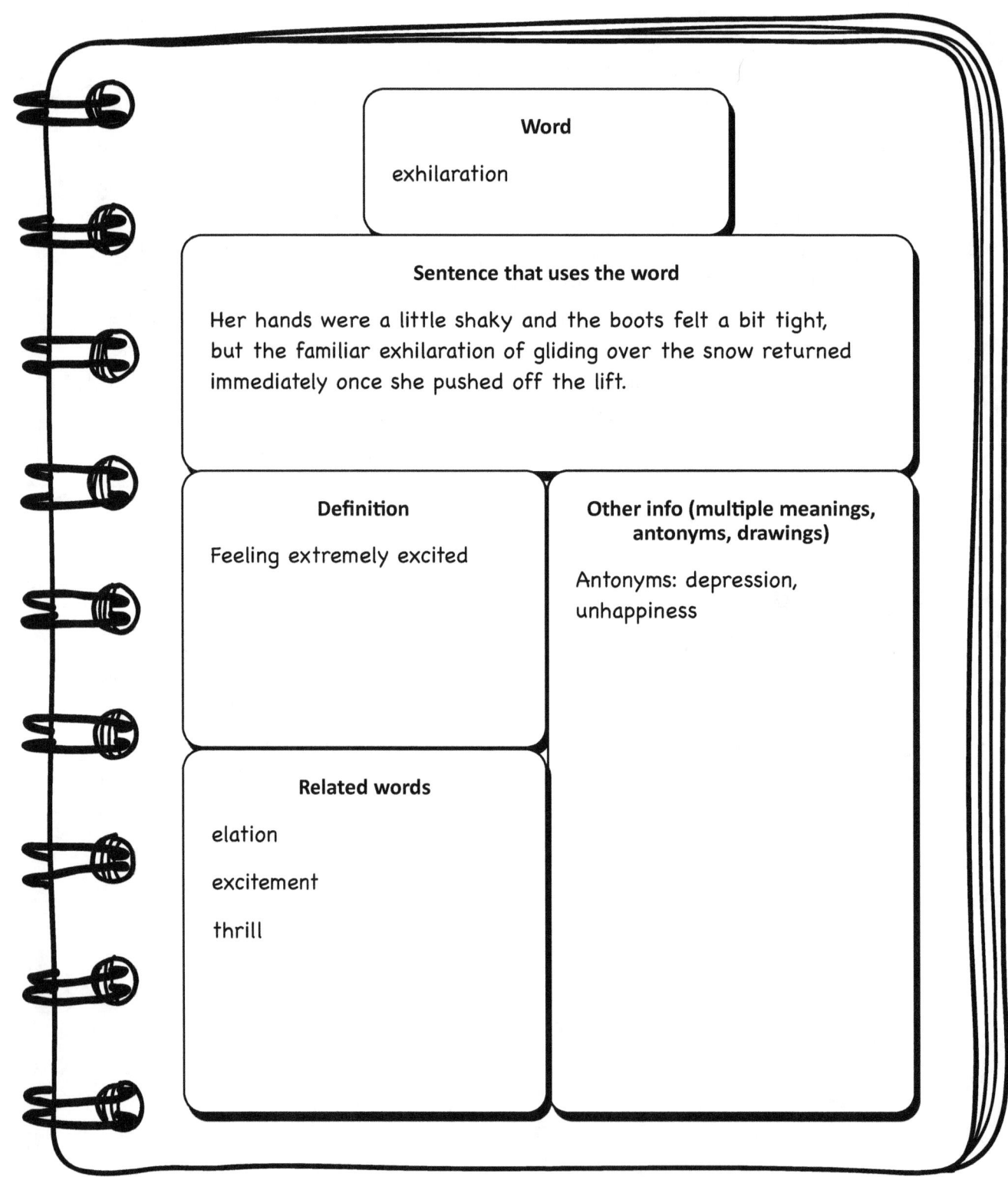

Name: _____ Date: _____

Word Nerd

Directions: Choose a new or interesting word from the text or discussion. Write about it.

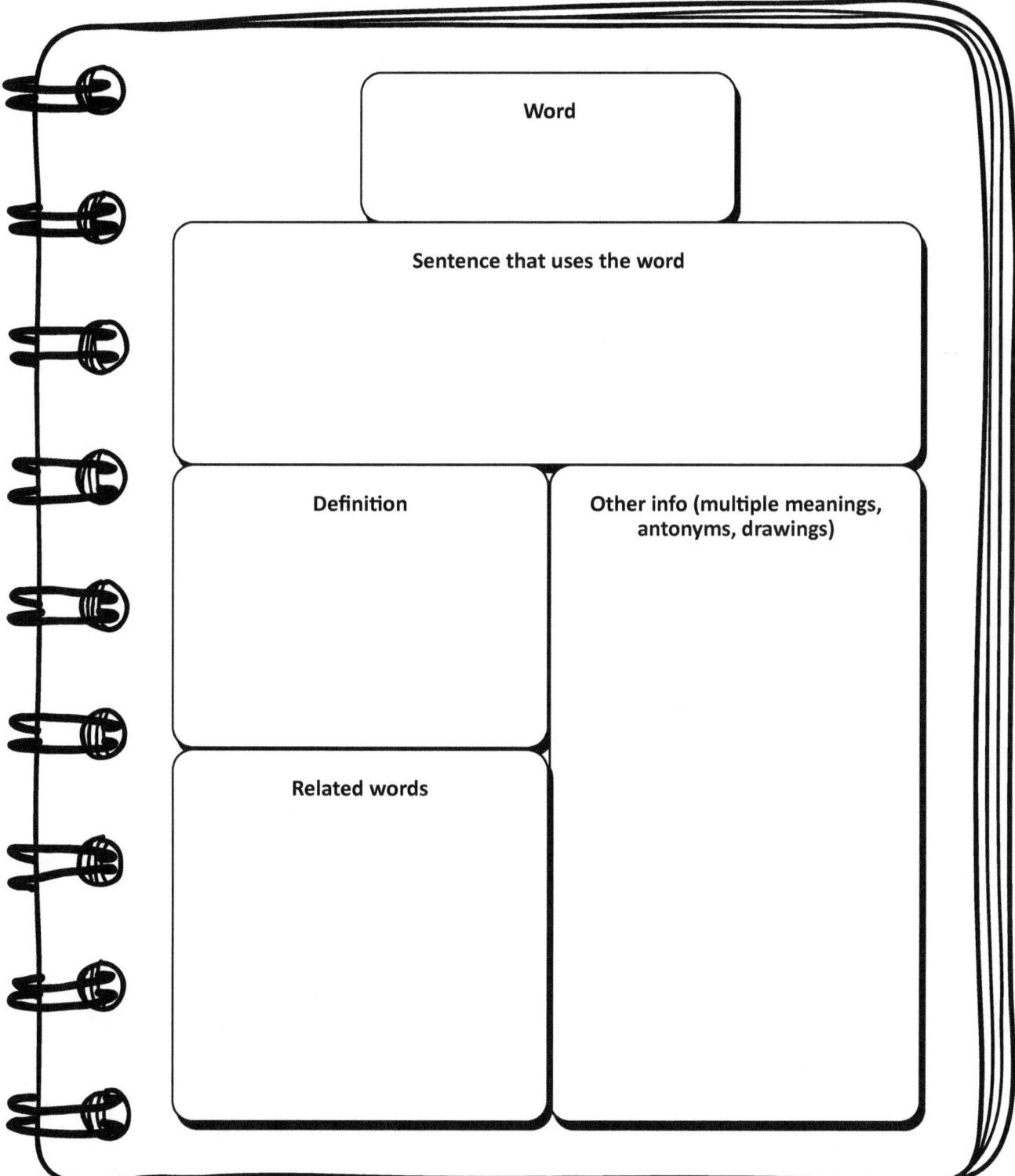

WORD RECOGNITION AND LANGUAGE KNOWLEDGE: MORPHOLOGY

Sort It Out

Objectives

- Use common, grade-appropriate Greek or Latin affixes and roots as clues to the meaning of a word.

Background Information

Sort It Out is a word sorting strategy that is excellent for teaching and reinforcing morphological and semantic analysis (Bear and Barone 1998; Bear et al. 2020; Templeton et al. 2015). Word sorts are a variation of semantic maps that students use to improve vocabulary, build categorization skills, and learn to organize concepts. Categorizing words helps readers build their understandings of patterns in words and form generalizations that help them recognize words. Readers later apply these generalizations to unknown words. In grades 6–12, pattern sorts are highly beneficial. Words can be sorted by common affixes, base words, and suffix spelling generalizations. Word sorts can be closed or open. In a closed sort, the teacher defines the sorting criteria (e.g., labeling the sort with specific prefix or suffix headings). In open sorts, students analyze the list of words to identify commonalities and then create the categories themselves.

Materials

- *Sort It Out* (page 43)

Process

1. Introduce a list of 10 to 20 words that share common affixes or bases. Read the words aloud, paying special attention to words that may be unfamiliar or difficult to pronounce.

2. Conduct a think-aloud to establish the categories for sorting. Model asking questions such as "What do I notice about these words?" or "What do some of these words have in common?" Alternately, as students become familiar with word sorts, invite them to generate the categories rather than conducting a think-aloud.

3. Provide students with *Sort It Out* activity sheets. Place students in pairs or small groups and have them discuss what the words have in common and how they will organize them. Students write the words in the categories they decided on and add category labels.

4. Bring students back together to review the sorts. Reflect on the categories and what the words had in common and review the meanings of the affixes or bases. Reinforce the groupings by paying attention to the categories and asking questions that allow students to verbalize their understanding.

Differentiation

- Give students the words in card format and have them physically sort the words on their desks or in notebooks.
- Word sorts can be made easier or more difficult for small group instruction. The number of categories can be increased or decreased; the contrast of the criteria can be made easier or more difficult; and the words chosen for the sort can be more or less complex depending on the number of affixes, lengths, morphemes, and the balance of familiar versus unfamiliar words.
- Word sorting by the focus criteria can be reinforced throughout the week by conducting "word hunts." Encourage students to record words from their textbooks, library books, and other reading material. They can also be encouraged to record words they hear in discussions or encounter in media. At the end of the week, place students in groups or pairs to share the words they found during the week.

Sort It Out Example

Words

bureaucrat
democracy
monocrat
theocratic
bureaucracy
autocrat
democrat
autocratic
monocratic
theocracy
theocrat
democratic
bureaucratic
monocracy

My Word Sort

-cracy
bureaucracy
democracy
autocracy
theocracy
monocracy

-crat
bureaucrat
democrat
autocrat
theocrat
monocrat

-cratic
bureaucratic
democratic
autocratic
theocratic
monocratic

Name: _____ Date: _____

Sort It Out

Directions: In the box, list the words to sort. Find common word parts or related meanings. Sort the words into categories. Label each category.

Words	My Word Sort

© Shell Education

Word Matrix

Objectives
- Use common, grade-appropriate Greek or Latin affixes and roots as clues to the meaning of a word.

Background Information
Word Matrix (Bowers, Kirby, and Deacon 2010) is a generative morphology strategy to familiarize students with roots, which are important tools for understanding words. As students become more advanced readers, they will acquire a large store of prefixes and suffixes, and knowledge of Greek and Latin bases. Using this knowledge to read the many complex multisyllabic words found in text at the middle and secondary level and to build vocabulary knowledge is highly effective. Recognizing the word parts and associating words as part of word families that share common bases promotes this vocabulary development, can improve fluency, and has positive impacts on spelling. Finally, much of the content-area vocabulary in math, social studies, and science contains Greek or Latin roots, so knowledge of them enhances learning content vocabulary and related concepts.

Materials
- *Word Matrix* (page 47)

Process
1. Select a base word for the lesson.
2. Explain to students that most multisyllabic words are made up of different parts (morphemes or roots). We know these are affixes (prefixes and suffixes) and base words. These are the smallest parts of words that carry meaning and cannot be broken into smaller words or word parts. We can make new words by combining these parts in different ways and can figure out the word meanings by analyzing the parts.
3. Provide each student with a *Word Matrix* activity sheet. Provide the base word and have students write it in the middle section of the matrix. Review its meaning and pronunciation. Ask the students to share affixes that can be used with the base word and have students write prefixes in the left section and suffixes in the right section.
4. Model combining the word parts to make a new word. Discuss the meaning of the new word based on knowledge of the meaning of the word parts.
5. Have students work individually or in pairs to create lists of new words.

6. Review the new words as a class. Write them on the board so students can add any words they may not have made to their activity sheets. Select a few words and determine the meanings by examining the parts.

7. Encourage students to choose three of their words and write sentences that reflect the appropriate meaning. Have students share their sentences with partners.

Differentiation

You may wish to provide students with a completed *Word Matrix* to assist them in making lists of new words. If using a completed matrix, review the affixes and the base word during step 2. As students become more familiar with using the matrix, have them fill in the affix sections of the matrix on their own. After students are familiar with common affixes, introduce less common Latin prefixes, number prefixes, and assimilated prefixes. It is not necessary to fill out all the sections. Their use will depend on the word being studied. Word Matrix can also be used to make words with multiple prefixes and suffixes.

Word Matrix Example

Common prefixes in de	Greek/Latin base word struct (to build)	Common inflectional suffixes s ed ing
Less common prefixes con ob		Common derivational suffixes or ion ive

1. instruct
2. instructed
3. instruction
4. instructive
5. instructor
6. destructed
7. destructing
8. destruction
9. constructing
10. constructed
11. construction
12. obstruct
13. obstruction
14. deconstructed
15. deconstructing

Sentences

1. The construction site filled the whole block.
2. The mud slide and rocks obstructed the road.
3. I read the instructions before I played the game.

Name: _____ Date: _____

Word Matrix

Directions: Write the base word, prefixes, and suffixes. Use the word parts to create new words. List the new words. Choose three words and write a sentence using each one.

Common prefixes	**Greek/Latin base word**	**Common inflectional suffixes**
Less common prefixes		**Common derivational suffixes**

_____ _____
_____ _____
_____ _____
_____ _____
_____ _____
_____ _____

Sentences

1. _____

2. _____

3. _____

WORD RECOGNITION AND LANGUAGE KNOWLEDGE: MORPHOLOGY

DISSECT

Objectives

- Determine or clarify the meaning of unknown and multiple-meaning words and phrases based on grade-level reading and content, choosing flexibly from a range of strategies.
- Demonstrate independence in gathering vocabulary knowledge when considering a word or phrase important to comprehension or expression.

Background Information

DISSECT is a strategy first designed as an intervention for middle grade students experiencing reading difficulties (Lenz and Hughes 1990). It has since been shared and adapted in a variety of ways and is appropriate for all students as a strategy to break down multisyllabic words. The acronym DISSECT is a clever mnemonic that prompts students to apply morphological knowledge and other word analysis strategies to decode unfamiliar words. This strategy works best with multisyllabic words composed of affixes and base words and for decoding unfamiliar words in context. DISSECT is a flexible strategy that can be taught to the whole class, then used and reinforced during small-group instruction.

Materials

- *Steps to DISSECT* (page 50)

Process

1. Select or create several sentences that contain an unfamiliar or complex word. Write one of the sentences on the board and read it aloud to students.

2. Demonstrate having difficulty reading the word, but continue on to the end of the sentence. Go back to the word. Think aloud, asking yourself, "What is that word?" Explain that there are steps we can take when we don't recognize a word.

3. Distribute *Steps to DISSECT*. Introduce and explain DISSECT:

    D: Discover the context: You can read the entire sentence, moving past the unknown word. Using the context, try to predict the unknown word. If the predicted word doesn't match (doesn't help the sentence make sense), proceed to the next step.

    I: Isolate the prefix: Examine the first few letters of the word to identify any prefix you know and draw a box around it.

S: Separate the suffix: Examine the last few letters of the word to identify any suffix you know and draw a box around it.

S: Say the stem: Pronounce the stem of the word. If you recognize it, read the prefix, stem, and suffix together to decode the word. If you are unable to pronounce or identify the stem, go to the next step.

E: Examine the stem: In this step, students are taught to dissect the stem using knowledge of phonics rules. These can be simplified as "the rules of 2s and 3s."

> Rule 1: If the stem begins with a vowel, separate the first two letters; if the stem or any part of the stem begins with a consonant, separate the first three letters and pronounce the rest. Apply this rule until the end of the stem is reached.
>
> Rule 2: If the word is still unreadable, then apply the second rule: Take off the first letter and try rule 1 again.
>
> Rule 3: When two vowels are together, try out other rules of pronunciation. If you are still unable to pronounce the word, proceed to the next step.

C: Check: Check with someone else to ask what the word means and how it is pronounced.

T: Try the dictionary: Use a print or online dictionary to identify the word and use the pronunciation guide or audio file to pronounce it. Read the definition.

4. Model using DISSECT with additional sentences. Next, have students practice in pairs, thinking aloud as they work through the steps with their partners.
5. Have students keep *Steps to DISSECT* in their notebooks as a reference.

Differentiation

Teach students how to use DISSECT over successive lessons. As students' knowledge of words and word parts such as affixes and base words advances, their ability to apply DISSECT will improve. Repeated modeling followed by practice during whole-group and small-group instruction will gradually lead to increased independence in using DISSECT. Challenge students with advanced vocabulary skills to replace the target word in each sentence with a related word and use the DISSECT procedure to break the replacement words apart.

Name: _____ Date:_____

Steps to DISSECT

D	Discover the context.	Read the entire sentence, moving past the unknown word. Using the context, try to predict the unknown word. If the predicted word doesn't match (doesn't help the sentence make sense), go to the next step.
I	Isolate the prefix.	Examine the first few letters of the word to identify any prefix you know and draw a box around it.
S	Separate the suffix.	Examine the last few letters of the word to identify any suffix you know and draw a box around it.
S	Say the stem.	Pronounce the stem of the word. If you recognize it, say the prefix, stem, and suffix together. If you are unable to pronounce the stem, go to the next step.
E	Examine the stem.	1. If the stem or part of the stem begins with a vowel, separate the first two letters and pronounce. If it begins with a consonant, separate the first three letters and pronounce. Continue to apply the rule until the end of the stem is reached. 2. If the word is still unreadable, take off the first letter and try rule 1 again. 3. When two vowels are together, use what you know about pronunciation. If you cannot identify the word, go to the next step.
C	Check.	Check with someone else to ask what the word means and how it is pronounced.
T	Try the dictionary.	Look up the word, use the pronunciation guide, and read the definition.

WORD RECOGNITION AND LANGUAGE KNOWLEDGE: SYNTAX AND SEMANTICS

Sentence Combining

Objectives

- Demonstrate command of the conventions of standard English grammar and usage when writing or speaking.

Background Information

Sentence Combining is an effective way to teach students to understand word order (syntax) and reinforce grammar skills in grades 6–12. In this strategy, students are taught to combine simple sentences into longer, grammatically complex sentences. Teaching students to write complex sentences improves the quality of their writing, enhances mastery of grammatical skills and concepts, and provides the opportunity for grammar practice in context rather than isolation (Graham and Perin 2007). Sentence Combining can be used to teach punctuation, tense and number agreement, parts of speech, conjunctions, and clauses. Sentence Combining should be taught explicitly with a focus on a particular grammatical concept for students to practice while developing these more complex sentences. Sentence Combining can be used across the curriculum as students practice and develop skills using the language of the disciplines.

Materials

- Sentence Combining activity sheet (created by teacher)

Process

1. Select a specific grammar concept for the focus of sentence combining. For example, the focus might be coordinating conjunctions (and, but) or subordinating conjunctions (after, until, unless).

2. Create a Sentence Combining activity sheet that targets the grammar concept. See page 52 for an example.

3. Introduce the lesson by defining and discussing the grammar concept.

4. Model combining two simple, short sentences using the concept. Display the original sentences and the combined sentences. Explain the reasoning for decisions you make while combining. For example, repetitive terms can be eliminated, or key phrases that indicate order of events or dependency are included.

5. Distribute copies of the Sentence Combining activity sheet. Have students work with partners to combine sets of sentences.

6. Have several pairs of students share their combined sentences with the class and explain their thinking.

7. Direct students to complete the activity sheet independently.

8. Have students share their combined sentences.

Differentiation

This process can be repeated with multiple variations of sentences and grammar concepts. Common areas of difficulty for students are writing sentences that are too simple, overuse of the word "and," run-on sentences, and repetitive sentence types. These can be addressed through sentence combining as a whole class or in small groups. Students may benefit from identifying sentences in their own writing to use for sentence combining. Challenge students by providing more complex sentences or having students independently select text sentences to combine.

Example

This example is for coordinating conjunctions using FANBOYS (for, and, nor, but, or, yet, so).

Original sentences: The motivational speaker visited our school. She gave a long speech.
New sentence: *The motivational speaker visited our school and gave a long speech.*

Original sentences: The students were excited to listen to the speaker. It was extremely hot that day and they were sitting outside.
New sentence: *The students were excited to listen to the speaker, but it was extremely hot that day and they were sitting outside.*

Original sentences: There was no shade outside. They did not have anything cold to drink.
New sentence: *There was no shade outside, nor did they have anything cold to drink.*

Original sentences: The crowd was getting restless. The began to whisper and fidget in their seats.
New sentence: *The crowd was getting restless, so they began to whisper and fidget in their seats.*

Original sentences: The speaker noticed the crowd moving. She kept talking.
New sentence: *The speaker noticed the crowd moving, yet she kept talking.*

Grammar Rants

Objectives

- Demonstrate understanding of figurative language, word relationships, and nuances in word meanings.

Background Information

The phrase *grammar rants* refers to passionate expressions found in blogs, memes, comment sections, and social media about the "incorrect" use of language or grammar. Dunn and Lindblom (2011) recommend analyzing grammar rants as a creative and engaging way to teach grammar to students. Students examine a published "rant" and analyze the author's complaint and the corresponding grammar rule or concept. Teachers and students can engage in discussions of "correct" and "incorrect" use of language, using language appropriate to an audience and context, and cultural shifts in language use. Teachers of higher grades can add an element of critical analysis, inviting students to comment on bias in the rant through the lens of race, class, age, and so on. Teaching grammar and language awareness through grammar rants is effective because it is interesting and engaging, students typically remember them, and grammar rants often focus on less complicated but very important aspects of language use that tend to hold social significance (Dunn and Lindblom 2011).

Materials

- *Grammar Rant* (page 56)
- one or more grammar rants

Process

1. Select a grammar rant for use with students. Grammar rants can be found online by searching "grammar rants" or "grammar memes." For published rants, see Dunn and Lindblom's *Grammar Rants: How a Backstage Tour of Writing Complaints Can Help Students Make Informed, Savvy Choices About Their Writing.*

2. Introduce the term "pet peeve." Explain that a pet peeve is something that is a minor annoyance to many people, but extremely annoying to a particular person. Explain that making simple grammatical errors can be a pet peeve for certain people, so much so that they choose to write about it! These writings are known as *grammar rants*.

3. Display the preselected grammar rant. Read it aloud or give students a few moments to read it to themselves.

4. Have students discuss the central complaint of the grammar rant with partners.

5. Provide each student with a *Grammar Rant* activity sheet. Lead a class discussion to analyze the grammar rant. Ask questions such as these:

   What is the ranter's pet peeve?

   Why does this annoy the ranter?

   Does this error interfere with meaning?

   Do you detect any bias?

   Do you have additional comments or thoughts about this rant?

6. Have students complete the reflection prompt at the bottom of the *Grammar Rant* activity sheet and share their reflections with partners or the whole class.

Foster critical analysis skills by encouraging students to think about any language-related biases that may be embedded in the rant. For example, perhaps the complaint reflects a cultural shift, such as older and younger people using language or applying grammatical concepts differently. The complaint might center on word or grammar choices that vary according to racial or class lines, or it might refer to a mistake made by English language learners. The rant might focus on ways people use language in different contexts, for example when texting versus other forms of writing. Other grammar rants may have roots in "hypercorrectness," which occurs when a writer or speaker tries to appear overly formal or well educated but excessively or incorrectly applies a grammatical concept, often producing unnatural-sounding language patterns.

Differentiation

Grammar rants selected for instruction should be chosen with great consideration paid to the grade level and maturity of students. This is meant to be a whole-class activity. Differentiate as needed by providing additional lessons that address the targeted grammar skill.

Grammar Rant Example

Grammar Pet Peeve	The ranter's pet peeve is when people use the preposition "on" instead of "in" to talk about boarding a plane.
What is annoying the ranter?	The ranter says you are going inside a plane, not getting on top of it.
Does it interfere with meaning?	Not really
Do you detect any bias?	I think this is hypercorrectness because almost everyone says "on" for transportation like buses, planes, and boats.
Additional Comments	Why do we say "in a car" not "on a car," but we say "on" for everything else?
What did you learn from this grammar rant? Explain.	I learned I could definitely think about how I use "in" and "on." Even though both are correct in this example, sometimes we just prefer one way over another way, and everyone still understands what you mean.

Name: _____ Date: _____

Grammar Rant

Directions: Read and analyze the grammar rant.

Grammar Pet Peeve	
What is annoying the ranter?	
Does it interfere with meaning?	
Do you detect any bias?	
Additional Comments	
What did you learn from this grammar rant? Explain.	

SECTION II:
Reading Comprehension and Content Knowledge

The strategies in this section correspond with key competencies identified in *What the Science of Reading Says about Reading Comprehension and Content Knowledge* (Jump and Kopp 2023). These research-based instructional strategies will help teachers bridge the gap between the science of literacy instruction and classroom practice.

Strategy	Skills and Understandings Addressed			
	Building Content Knowledge	Text Structures and Verbal Reasoning	Comprehension Strategies	Discussion-Based Comprehension Strategies
Anticipation Guide	■			
Collaborative Concept Map	■			
Text Structure Analysis		■		
Text Analysis Pyramid		■		
Annotation			■	
Annotate and Compare			■	
Structured Annotation			■	
Line-by-Line Reading			■	
GRASP			■	

Strategy	Skills and Understandings Addressed *(cont.)*			
	Building Content Knowledge	Text Structures and Verbal Reasoning	Comprehension Strategies	Discussion-Based Comprehension Strategies
Thinking at Right Angles			■	
Question Journal			■	
Facts-Questions-Responses (FQR)			■	
Get the GIST			■	
Double Entry Journal			■	
Reciprocal Teaching				■
Text Rendering				■

Reading Comprehension and Content Knowledge

Simply put, reading comprehension is understanding what is read. It is the knowledge that words represent thoughts and ideas. It is the skill required for meaning-making, and meaning-making is the very heart of reading. Why read words if we cannot make meaning from them? While we may be able to define reading comprehension simply, the act is not so simple. Researchers from a variety of disciplines have attempted to describe, visualize, theorize, and model the processes that occur in a reader's mind when making meaning from words, and while there may not be a definitive model, there is much we have learned that has significant implications for instructional practices.

In order to comprehend what they read, readers must have strong foundational skills. They must have the ability to accurately and effortlessly decode most or all of the words in a text (Duke, Ward, and Pearson 2021). We know readers must be able to cognitively process the words, drawing meaning from their own experiences and knowledge to understand the author's message. Many agree that reading is a dialogue between the reader and the author, and during this dialogue, the reader generates questions to help anticipate meaning, search for information, respond intellectually and emotionally, and infer ideas from and explain further the content of the text.

> Readers must be able to cognitively process the words, drawing meaning from their own experiences and knowledge to understand the author's message.

Many adolescent readers come prepared with the foundational skills of decoding and fluency. While decoding and fluency skills are necessary components for reading comprehension, it is widely accepted that they are not sufficient. In grades 6–12, reading comprehension instruction is vitally important to content area learning and continued academic success. Literacy demands in these grades change significantly. The texts students encounter are longer, and the words and sentences are more complex. Adolescent readers must be able to effectively negotiate increased structural complexity and more sophisticated conceptual knowledge in order to access meaning in and across texts. Additionally, as content area instruction becomes more discipline-specific and specialized, texts do the same. The types of texts vary greatly, requiring students to have a complex set of metacognitive skills, which need to be further developed in grades 6–12 through explicit instruction. These include generalized comprehension skills learned in previous grades, which many students may still need to practice. These skills include setting a purpose for reading, activating background knowledge, making inferences, summarizing text, and synthesizing concepts within texts. The disciplinary nature of reading in grades 6–12 requires specialized explicit instruction in word use, language, text, and discourse structures specific to math, science, social studies, and English language arts. Students also benefit from continued development of verbal reasoning skills, academic talk, and discussion-based approaches to comprehension instruction.

Navigating Text for Comprehension

Decades of research have helped us determine what effective readers do as they read (National Reading Panel 2000). Some of the most interesting findings came from the work of Pressley and Afflerbach (1995), in which proficient readers explained what was happening in their minds while reading by thinking aloud to the researchers. From this and other studies, we have learned that good readers have pre-reading behaviors that include setting a purpose for reading and previewing text to take note of organizational patterns and text structure. Proficient readers draw from their prior knowledge to predict events and information, generate hypotheses as they read, and determine the meaning of unknown words or confusing phrases. They make inferences, make connections between ideas and texts, draw conclusions, and summarize. These readers ask themselves questions throughout the reading process. If we wanted to summarize these behaviors into one sentence, we would be correct in stating that *proficient readers are strategic readers*.

It stands to reason that secondary teachers can develop readers by providing strategy instruction to model and scaffold behaviors of strategic reading. Reading comprehension strategies have been defined as cognitive and metacognitive processes readers use deliberately and consciously for the means of understanding what they are reading (Almasi and Hart 2018; Paris, Lipson, and Wixson 1983; Pressley, Borkowski, and Schneider 1987). The following strategies assist students in navigating complex text in grades 6–12 (Fisher, Frey, and Almarode 2022):

- self-questioning strategies to predict, resolve problems, and clarify understanding
- summarizing strategies to discern and connect key ideas, and to reduce content to reflect essential understanding
- inferencing strategies to connect text evidence to prior knowledge and experiences in ways that enhance understanding
- self-monitoring strategies to recognize when they have lost meaning in a text and strategies to restore meaning
- connection strategies to integrate reader experience and the information being read
- analysis strategies to identify literary devices, determine the author's purpose, and critically evaluate texts

> Reading comprehension strategies have been defined as cognitive and metacognitive processes that readers use deliberately and consciously for the means of understanding what they are reading.

READING COMPREHENSION AND CONTENT KNOWLEDGE

Strategy instruction is a critical component of adolescent literacy instruction. However, it is important to note that it is just one component of comprehension instruction and research does not recommend teaching strategies in isolation. We teach strategies because we have learned they represent the behaviors of strategic readers. Therefore, strategy instruction is not meant to teach readers to use a strategy but to teach them to be strategic. Almasi and Hart describe why this distinction is important: "The difference [between teaching students a 'strategy' versus teaching students to be 'strategic'] is that strategic actions require intentionality—they require a reader who is actively processing the text and making decisions about it" (2018, 228). Instruction that scaffolds students' selection of appropriate strategies, embeds strategy instruction, and involves multiple strategies is most effective.

The Role of Discussion in Comprehension

Effective middle and high school classrooms provide opportunities for students to further their academic oral language and discourse skills. Research demonstrates that students who engage in quality discussions of the meaning and interpretation of texts improve their reading comprehension of complex text. During quality discussions, students can sharpen these skills and overall comprehension as they express their own interpretations of text, have their positions challenged, defend their positions, and listen as others defend positions (Kamil et al. 2008). During discussions, teachers model questioning, reasoning, and interpreting texts, and students have the opportunity to listen to multiple examples of how meaning is constructed as teachers and peers participate.

> Research demonstrates that students who engage in quality discussions of the meaning and interpretation of texts improve their reading comprehension of complex text.

Classroom discussions can be undertaken with whole group, in small groups, or between pairs of students. The teacher does not need to be the leader or center of the conversation; however, quality discussions require planning and often scaffolding to guide questioning, response, and the exchange of ideas.

When designing discussion activities around text, teachers should consider specific goals for the discussion or discussion-based tasks, and explain and support students in applying the rules and procedures that facilitate effective discussions, such as reaching consensus, listening to opposing ideas, and moving the group forward (Fisher, Frey, and Almarode 2022).

The Role of Content Knowledge in Comprehension

Since the ultimate goal is to produce competent, independent, strategic readers, we must address the needs of the whole reader and develop their capacities to know not just how but when to use strategies. If you review the description of the strategies above, you can't help but notice that several strategies rely on the reader activating and making connections to their background knowledge. Decades of reading research have shown that along with decoding and fluency skills, another key to reading comprehension is the development of a broad base of knowledge one can activate and apply to the reading situation. This knowledge includes topics we covered previously such as academic vocabulary, morphology, and familiarity with text and language structures, but it also includes topical knowledge. Wattenberg points out that "as students age and gain basic skills, the lack of knowledge typically becomes the much greater obstacle to good reading" (2016, 2).

A broad base of content or topical knowledge can give readers a comprehension advantage when they encounter a diversity of topics, particularly in science and social studies. Research demonstrates that having schema (relevant prior knowledge) for a topic aids not only in the comprehension process but also in the learning process. When a topic or concept is introduced in text and students can initiate the retrieval process (activating their schema for the topic), they have an anchor to which they can connect the new information to better understand it (Anderson and Pearson 1984). If we think of our schema as a set of folders in a filing cabinet (or in our "cloud storage"), it is easier for us to add items to our existing folders than it is to create a whole new folder with a whole new label and find things to fill it with. This is an overly simplistic but helpful analogy for thinking about the importance of schema. The advantage this broad knowledge bestows goes beyond the facts and information of a topic. When students have knowledge of facts, ideas, and concepts across content areas, they can develop an understanding of how concepts/topics are related, how they are explained, how processes work, and more—all essential skills for disciplinary literacy.

> When students have knowledge of facts, ideas, and concepts across content areas, they can develop an understanding of how concepts/topics are related, how they are explained, how processes work, and more.

Content and concept knowledge can facilitate incidental word learning. When students have knowledge of a concept or topic, it can allow them to better understand new vocabulary or technical vocabulary related to that concept. This knowledge of related words can activate broader semantic networks (the organization of facts and knowledge in the mind) to enhance comprehension and accelerate new learning (Cervetti, Wright, and Hwang 2016; Willingham 2006). Concept and content knowledge will also assist readers in understanding

READING COMPREHENSION AND CONTENT KNOWLEDGE

words with multiple meanings. For example, exposure to and broad knowledge of marine life can help a reader distinguish the differing meanings of the word *school*, as in a *school of fish* as opposed to an *elementary school*. Similarly, familiarity with a topic can help students understand figurative language, be able to distinguish that a statement is indeed figurative and not literal, and interpret the meaning of the figurative statement. For example, students read that a team of scientists really "hit it out of the park" with the results of their latest study. Exposure to or familiarity with baseball would help one understand (1) this is a figurative statement—the scientists did not actually hit anything and an actual park was not involved—and (2) the scientists' results were significant and considered remarkable.

The recommendations for supporting content learning are complementary to those for teaching reading comprehension. It is not possible that we could teach students all of the facts, information, and concepts they are likely to encounter in every piece of text! Therefore, isolated instruction is not beneficial. Embedded strategy instruction is the key. Embedding this instruction in a wide variety of text genres and providing exposure to multiple texts develops layers and depth of knowledge. Building a broad base of content knowledge is part of the push for an increase in the amount of informational text students engage with during elementary school, in recognition of the benefits to students as they transition to middle and high school. Students in grades 6–12 continue to access and develop this broad base of content knowledge while at the same time deepening their knowledge of specific concepts and ideas and the relationships between them. Teachers can design instruction that includes both knowledge building activities and those that facilitate depth of understanding. Instruction in an even greater variety of genres and text structures—furthering student's knowledge of organizational patterns, language structures, and knowledge across domains—is crucial.

> Instruction in an even greater variety of genres and text structures—furthering student's knowledge of organizational patterns, language structures, and knowledge across domains—is crucial.

The strategies in this chapter are intended to develop competent, independent, and strategic readers who can understand and learn from a diversity of texts across a wide variety of topics. This type of reader can flexibly and independently employ various strategies when reading, making decisions about which strategies to use and switching between strategies when necessary. Great teachers know that some strategies work for some students and other strategies work for other students, just as some strategies work best with certain types of reading material and other strategies work best with other types of reading material. The most important thing to remember when trying to improve reading comprehension in students is that the skill level, group dynamic, and makeup of students should determine the approach to take and which modifications to lessons may be needed.

Anticipation Guide

Objectives

- Cite textual evidence to support analysis of what the text says explicitly, as well as inferences drawn from the text.
- Determine a central idea of a text and how it is conveyed through particular details; provide a summary of the text distinct from personal opinions or judgments.
- Analyze in detail how a key individual, event, or idea is introduced, illustrated, and elaborated in a text.

Background Information

Anticipation Guides are designed to stimulate students' thinking about a topic, concept, or idea before they begin a unit or engage with a text (Kozen, Murray, and Windell 2006). They encourage students to express opinions, make connections to previous knowledge, and make predictions about the topic they will study. A variation incorporates multimedia resources such as websites or video or audio clips, and focuses students on engaging with the content rather than being passive observers. Using a text or multimedia resource supports building background knowledge by both activating knowledge students may have and frontloading information for students with limited or surface knowledge of a topic. Students first take a position on several statements. They engage with the resource and then respond to the statements again, using their new knowledge to support their responses. Anticipation Guides help set a purpose for engaging with text or multimedia as students view or listen to find information that supports or challenges their positions.

Materials

- Anticipation Guide (created by teacher)
- text or multimedia resource on topic of study

Process

1. Identify a knowledge-building text or multimedia resource related to the topic of study and preview it to determine important concepts students should focus on. Prepare an anticipation guide of five to ten short statements about these concepts or ideas (see examples on page 67). The statements should be designed to activate prior knowledge students may have about the topic. Statements should also help establish a purpose for reading the text. True/false or agree/disagree statements work best. Present the statements in the order in which the ideas appear in the resource.

2. Distribute the Anticipation Guide to students before they engage with the text or multimedia selection and allow time for students to read the statements and respond in the "Before" column.

3. Hold a class discussion, asking students to share their responses.

4. Have students engage with the text or multimedia selection as a class, individually, or with partners as appropriate. Tell students they should look or listen for evidence that supports or refutes their "Before" responses. Have students complete the "After" column on the guide as they discover evidence.

5. Engage in a collaborative discussion about the "After" answers, asking students to explain their thinking. Ask students if they changed their responses as a result of the text or multimedia resource, and have them share evidence they found.

Differentiation

- With new or particularly challenging topics, you may wish to scaffold learning by preparing stopping points in the resource, guiding students step by step through the content in smaller chunks. Alternately, students can work in groups to respond to the anticipation guide after they engage with the resource.

- This activity can be extended by having students write about whether their new learning supports their "Before" opinions, citing evidence from the resource. Students should be encouraged to disagree with information they heard if they can successfully create an argument and support it with details.

Example of a True/False Anticipation Guide

Before		Statement	After	
True	False		True	False
		The Supreme Court is the head of the judicial branch. Evidence:		
		Supreme Court judges can serve a maximum of 25 years. Evidence:		
		There are nine justices on the Supreme Court. Evidence:		
		A Supreme Court ruling can be appealed to the Executive or Legislative Branch of the government. Evidence:		
		The Supreme Court accepts most of the cases that come before it. Evidence:		

COMPREHENSION: BUILDING CONTENT KNOWLEDGE

Collaborative Concept Map

Objectives

- Determine the central ideas or information of grade-level concepts and demonstrate understanding of relationships between these ideas and concepts.

Background Information

Creating a Collaborative Concept Map provides students the opportunity to step back from their individual perspectives and draw from the knowledge of peers and the power of the multiple perspectives. Concept maps are diagrams that show the relationships between concepts and ideas. They help students store, organize, and develop a broad base of content knowledge. Creating concept maps in small groups helps students generate meaningful conversations about content. Collaborative Concept Maps can be used to generate discussion prior to reading as a way to build conceptual knowledge, after initial exposure to a topic to make connections, or after reading to organize and summarize content learning.

Materials

- text selection

Process

1. Review the material students will be reading. List the important concepts in the reading, and note other concepts, words, and phrases that are related to these concepts. Have this list on hand to help guide students' discussions.

2. Explain to students that concept maps show relationships between ideas and concepts. Pose a question or provide a topic as the subject of the concept map.

3. Arrange students in small groups and have them work together to generate a list of words and ideas that are related to the topic. It may be useful to provide a complete or partial list of the ideas and concepts you developed (see step 1).

4. Provide each group with chart paper. One student writes the question or topic in the center of the map. Next, students discuss the relationships between the key ideas and make decisions about how this information should be represented on the concept map. Then, students can begin adding and organizing information on their maps.

5. Have groups share and explain their concept maps with the class or with another group. Encourage students to compare, contrast, and justify the information on and organization of their concept maps with one another.

6. After sharing, give groups time to add to or revise their maps based on the discussion and feedback from other groups.

Differentiation

Scaffold the activity by providing a list of the ideas, words, and concepts to students. The focus of the concept mapping will be on how to organize this list to demonstrate understanding of the relationships between the ideas. It may be helpful for some students to color-code the relationships represented on the map. Provide challenge by encouraging students to make connections between new concepts and known concepts.

Concept Map Example

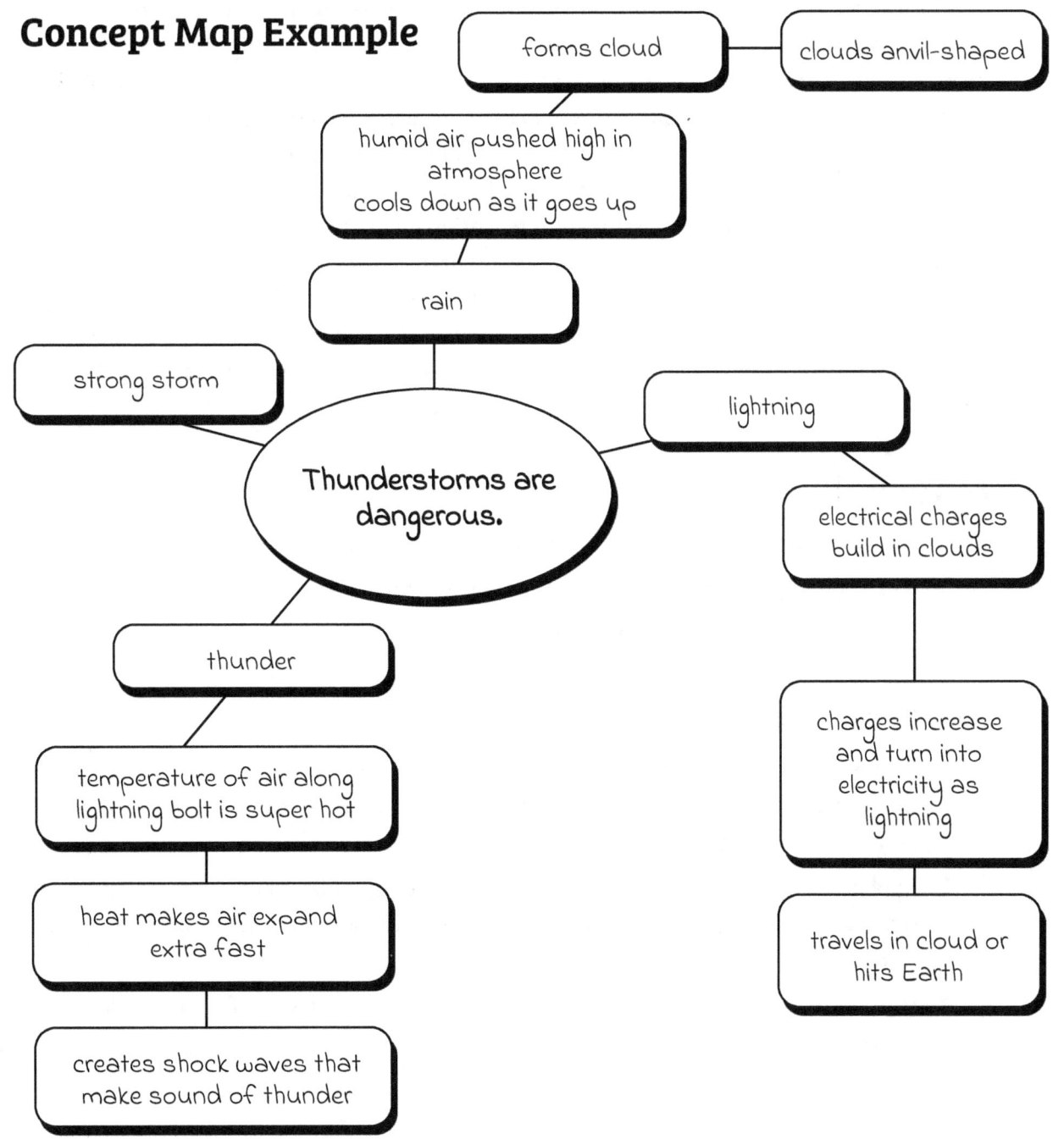

COMPREHENSION: TEXT STRUCTURES AND VERBAL REASONING

Text Structure Analysis

Objectives
- Analyze the structure an author uses to organize a text, including how the major sections contribute to the whole and to the development of the ideas.

Background Information
Text Structure Analysis teaches students to identify text structure to enhance comprehension of informational text. Text structure refers to the way authors organize information in text. This includes the arrangement of ideas and concepts and the relationships between them. Awareness of text structure includes an awareness of how language is used to expresses ideas, concepts, and relationships within a given text structure. As readers in grades 6–12 navigate complex text across content areas, knowledge of words and language patterns that signal text structure in text and in questions combined with knowledge of graphic organizers for notetaking provide students a path for comprehension and study of ideas and concepts. Students who analyze informational text for structural elements are more likely to learn from text (RAND 2003). The following lesson is based on Tompkins's (2001) steps for teaching informational text structure. This lesson can be followed an adapted to teach each type of text structure individually. There are five common text structures students should be familiar with (see page 73).

Materials
- text that models a specific text structure
- corresponding *Text Structure* graphic organizer (pages 74–78)
- *Text Structure Reference Guide* (page 73)

Process
1. Choose a text structure for the focus of the lesson. Select expository text that models this structure. Short paragraphs are appropriate for practice, though older students may be able to navigate longer text selections.
2. Explain that informational texts follow patterns of organization known as text structures. There are several common text structures, and knowledge of these can help readers understand and learn from the text.
3. Introduce the text structure students will examine in this lesson. Provide students with the corresponding *Text Structure* graphic organizer.

4. Display the sample text. Review the signal words and phrases, highlighting where these are found in the text. Demonstrate how these signal words provide clues to the text structure the author is using and clues to how to organize notes.
5. Model how to use the graphic organizer for note-taking.
6. Give students time to analyze additional text for signal words and phrases. Have them continue to take notes on the graphic organizer.
7. Have students discuss their notes with partners.
8. Repeat the lesson over time for the other text structures. Students may need multiple lessons to become familiar with each one.

Differentiation

Students may benefit from repeated practice analyzing paragraphs or shorter pieces of text before moving on to textbook selections or other content-area reading materials. Students may also benefit from additional scaffolding by providing a completed graphic organizer or sentence frames for the written response. Students with intermediate or advanced knowledge of text structure should be encouraged to self-select the appropriate graphic organizers for note-taking if needed.

Examples of Common Signal Words

Text Structure	Signal Words	Graphic Organizer
cause-effect	as a result, as a consequence, because, brought about, consequently, due to, for, in order to, led to, since, so, that is why, the effect of, the outcome was, the reason was, therefore	

(continued)

Examples of Common Signal Words *(cont.)*

Text Structure	Signal Words	Graphic Organizer
compare-contrast	also, although, as opposed to, as well as, both, different, however, like, much as, not only…but also, on the contrary, on the other hand, same, similar(ly), too, yet	(Venn diagram)
description	all, for example, for instance, in addition, in fact, most(ly), some, specifically, such as, to illustrate, too	(cluster/web diagram)
problem-solution	answer, challenge, conclusion, dilemma, fortunately, issue, led to, one challenge, problem, question, solved, therefore, trouble, unfortunately	(problem-solution boxes with arrows)
sequence of events	after, before, during, eventually, finally, first, following, immediately, in the end, last(ly), meanwhile, next, now, then, when, while	(flow chart)

Name: _____ Date:_____

Text Structure Reference Guide

Description

The information about a topic (object, person, animal, idea, event) includes facts, characteristics, traits, and features.

Example: description of national symbols

Cause and Effect

The information is presented to make clear that certain things (effects) happen as a result of other things (causes).

Example: causes and consequences of the Civil War

Sequence

The facts, events, or concepts are presented in sequential order. The topic is developed in order of importance, or the sequence or steps in a process are given.

Example: the evolution of language and its written forms

Problem and Solution

The development of a problem and possible solutions to it are presented.

Example: conflicts between American Indian tribes and the government and possible solutions

Compare and Contrast

The similarities (comparison) and differences (contrast) among facts, people, events, and concepts are presented.

Example: transportation of the past vs. transportation of today

Name: _____ Date: _____

Text Structure: Description

Directions: Review the text structure and signal words. Write examples you find in the text. Record notes about the text on the graphic organizer.

Description

The author writes about a topic, idea, person, place, or thing by explaining its features, characteristics, facts, or examples.

Signal Words

all	in fact	such as
for example	most(ly)	to illustrate
for instance	some	too
in addition	specifically	

Words I Found

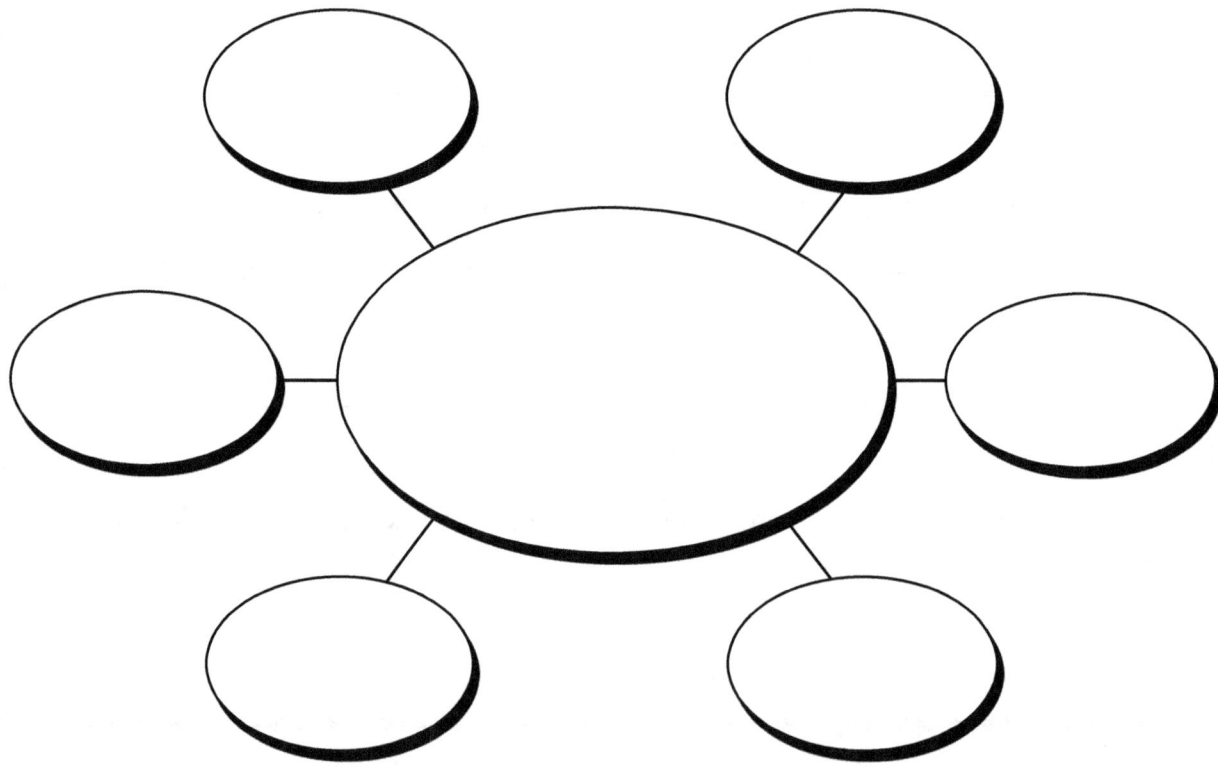

Name: _____ Date: _____

Text Structure: Sequence

Directions: Review the text structure and signal words. Write examples you find in the text. Record notes about the text on the graphic organizer.

Sequence

The author describes the order of events or steps in a process and lists them in chronological or numerical order.

Signal Words

after	finally	in the end	now
before	first	last(ly)	then
during	following	meanwhile	when
eventually	immediately	next	while

Words I Found

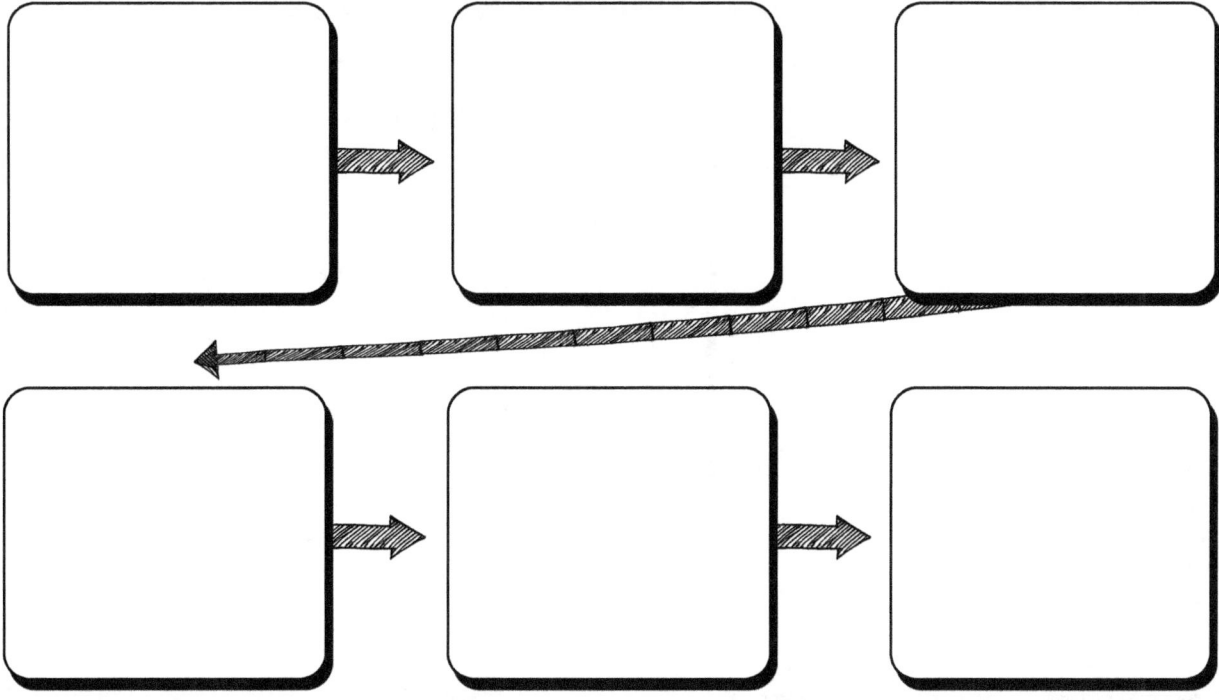

Name: _____ Date: _____

Text Structure: Cause and Effect

Directions: Review the text structure and signal words. Write examples you find in the text. Record notes about the text on the graphic organizer.

Cause and Effect

The purpose is to explain how or why something happens. The author explains the causes, or events, and the effects, results, or consequences of the events.

Signal Words

as a consequence	due to	that is why
as a result	for	the effect of
because	in order to	the outcome was
brought about	led to	the reason was
consequently	since	therefore
	so	

Words I Found

Causes

Effects

Name: _____ Date:_____

Text Structure: Compare and Contrast

Directions: Review the text structure and signal words. Write examples you find in the text. Record notes about the text on the graphic organizer.

Compare and Contrast

The author explains how two or more things are alike and how they are different.

Signal Words

also	both	not only… but also	same
although	different	on the contrary	similar(ly)
as opposed to	however	on the other hand	too
as well as	like		yet
	much as		

Words I Found

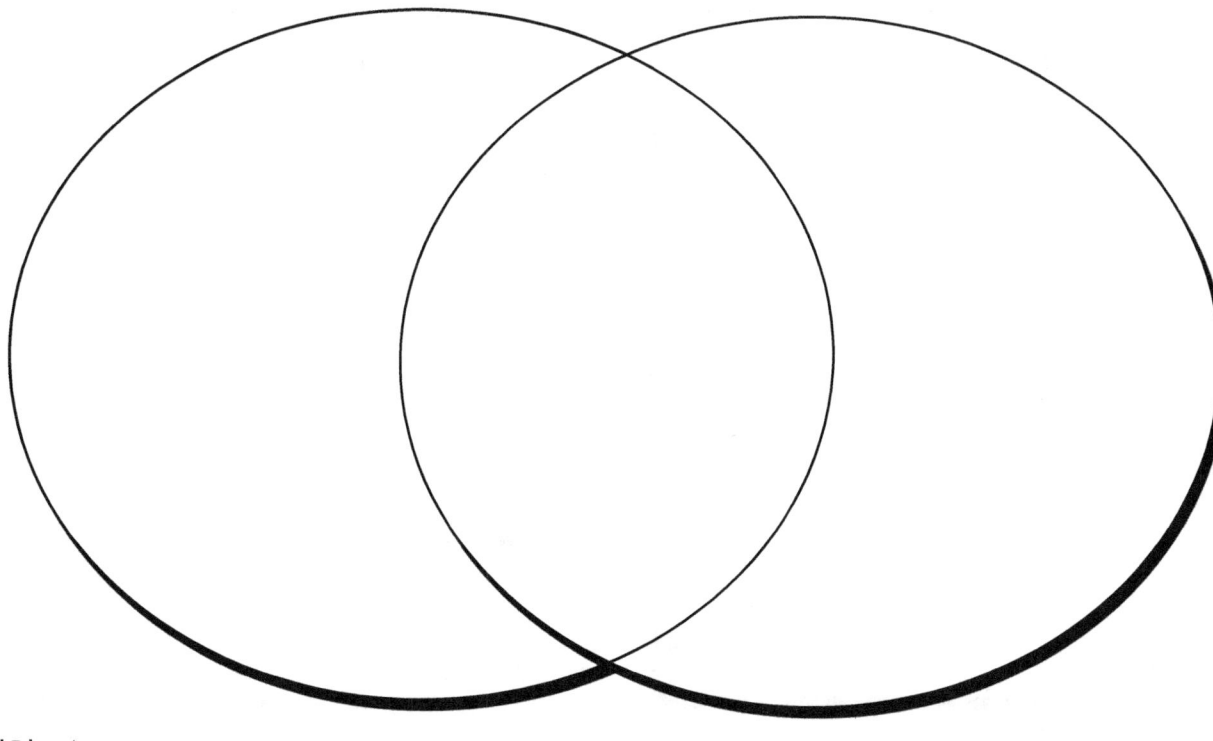

Name: _____ Date: _____

Text Structure: Problem and Solution

Directions: Review the text structure and signal words. Write examples you find in the text. Record notes about the text on the graphic organizer.

Problem and Solution

The author describes a problem and one or more potential solutions to the problem.

Signal Words

answer	issue	solved
challenge	led to	therefore
conclusion	one challenge	trouble
dilemma	problem	unfortunately
fortunately	question	

Words I Found

Problem  **Solutions**

COMPREHENSION: TEXT STRUCTURES AND VERBAL REASONING

Text Analysis Pyramid

Objectives
- Analyze the structure an author uses to organize a text, including how the major sections contribute to the whole and to the development of ideas.

Background Information
Analyzing text structure helps students focus on the most important ideas in a text and enhances comprehension of a text. Text structure refers to the way authors organize information in text. This includes the arrangement of ideas and concepts and the relationships between them. Awareness of text structure includes an awareness of how language is used to express ideas, concepts, and relationships within a given text structure. Students who analyze information text for structural elements are more likely to learn from text (RAND 2003).

Materials
- text that models a specific text structure
- *Text Analysis Word Pyramid* (page 81)

Process
1. Choose a text that models an expository text structure. Short paragraphs are appropriate for practice, though older students may be able to navigate longer text selections.
2. Review the idea that informational texts follow patterns of organization known as text structures. There are several common text structures, and awareness of these can help readers understand and learn from the text.
3. Introduce the text structure students will examine in this lesson. Provide students with the *Text Analysis Word Pyramid*.
4. Display the sample text. Preview it with the students and ask students to identify important words or phrases. Have students choose a word or phrase and write it in the top section of the organizer. Invite a few volunteers to share what they wrote.
5. Repeat for the remaining sections of the pyramid, scaffolding the process of identifying the following: clues about the author's purpose, signal words that provide clues to the text structure, words that are important to the main idea, and words that indicate the mood or tone of the text.

6. Have students share their completed pyramids with partners.
7. Repeat the lesson over time for the other text structures.
8. After students have been taught to use the *Text Analysis Word Pyramid*, it may be used with other texts to support reading comprehension.

Differentiation

Students may benefit from repeated practice analyzing paragraphs or shorter pieces of text before moving on to textbook selections or other content area reading materials. Students may also benefit by working with small groups or partners to analyze a text.

Name: _____ Date: _____

Text Analysis Word Pyramid

Directions: Identify important words and phrases from the text. Record them in the organizer.

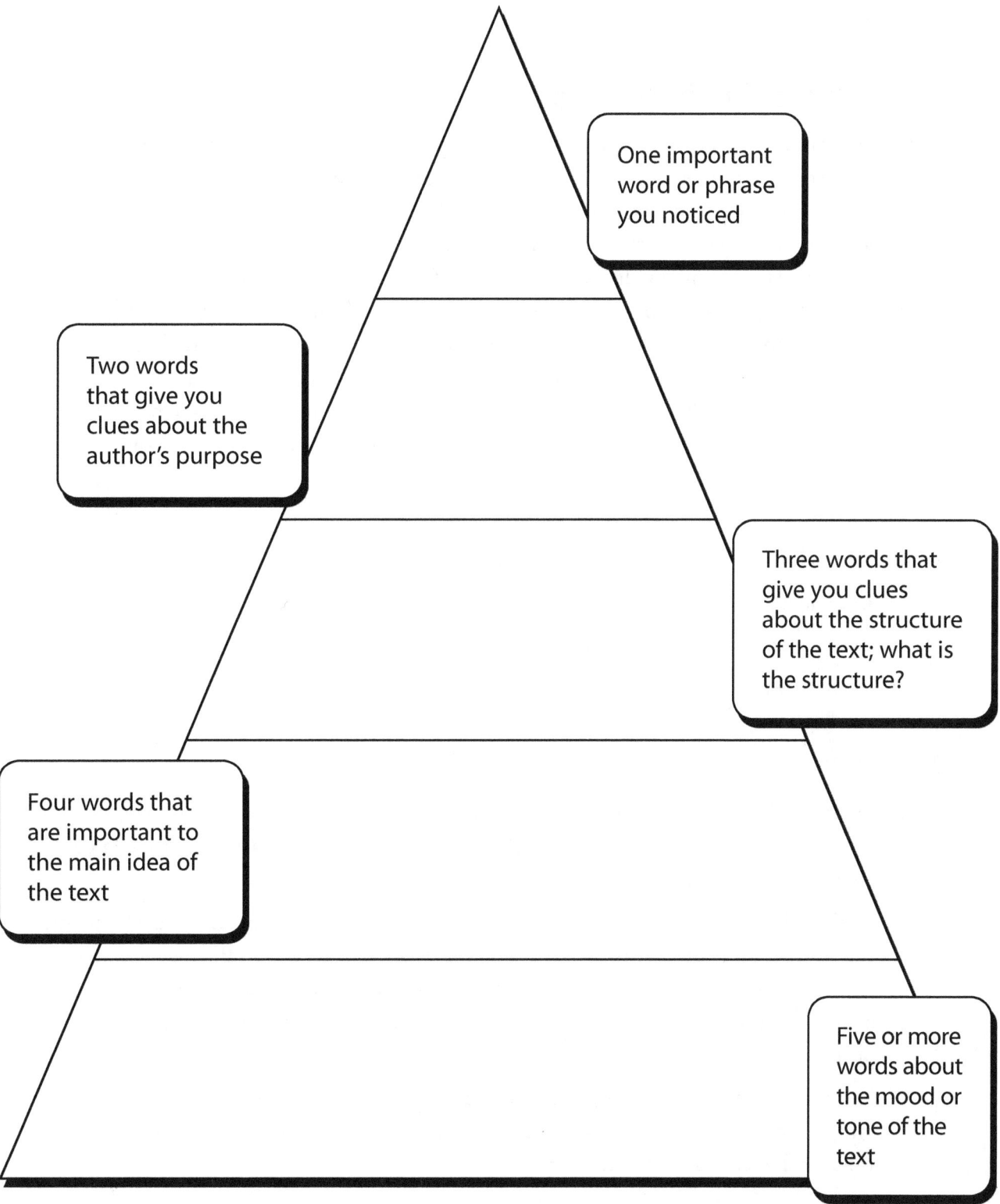

Annotation

Objectives

- Read closely to determine what the text says explicitly and to make logical inferences from it; cite specific textual evidence when writing or speaking to support conclusions drawn from the text.

Background Information

Annotation is a note-taking strategy that helps students stay engaged; track their thinking; and generate questions about, connect to, and better understand text. Annotation develops a sophisticated skill set: students practice thinking about important information and main ideas, monitor their understanding, summarize and synthesize in real time as they are reading, and later discuss with peers (Fisher and Frey 2014). Students annotate by "coding" text using markings or symbols to represent new information, points of confusion, connection, and so on. Students highlight unknown words, important facts, and questions they have. For narrative text, students can find and annotate evidence of character traits, or the theme, problem, or solution. In informational text, annotations can be made to track main ideas and key details or to make connections between visuals and diagrams and the body of the text.

Materials

- annotated text selection
- text selection and questions based on it
- sticky notes

Process

1. Prepare a short sample of complex text with annotations. The sample can focus on a particular purpose for annotation, such as questioning or summarizing, or it can be an example of a variety of annotations.

2. Explain that annotations enhance reading by making note of your thinking about the text as you read. Annotating involves making notes on a text or in the margins of a text or on sticky notes. They can include underlining or highlighting key information, but annotating is more than simply highlighting text. It is marking text for a specific purpose.

3. Distribute or display the sample text. Have students review the annotations on the sample. Lead the class in a discussion, prompting students to consider the use and value of the annotations in the sample.

4. Discuss specific annotations students may wish to use, such as the following.
   - Underline important information, main points
   - Circle key words, phrases, or points of confusion
   - Make a question mark for questions (tell students be sure to write their question)
   - Margin notes about things that are interesting or worthy of note
5. Assign students a text and give them time to read and practice annotating. After students annotate the text, have them share with partners, explaining their thinking and the significance of the annotations.
6. Have a class discussion and ask students to share their thinking about the text and annotations. Clarify misunderstandings or misapplication of annotating as needed.
7. Provide several text-based questions and have students use their annotations as a guide to finding the answers.

Differentiation

Some students may benefit from hearing the reading selection read aloud as they follow along and make annotations. Differentiate the use of annotations by simplifying the purpose for annotating or reducing the number of symbols students should use. Scaffold the process by having groups of three to five students work together in a shared digital document, annotating the same text. Encourage students with advanced reading skills to develop their own annotation keys with unique symbols that they find helpful to their reading.

COMPREHENSION: STRATEGIES

Annotate and Compare

Objectives
- Read closely to determine what the text says explicitly and to make logical inferences from it; cite specific textual evidence when writing or speaking to support conclusions drawn from the text.

Background Information
Annotate and Compare is a strategy for teaching readers the valuable skill of annotation. Annotation develops a sophisticated skill set: students practice thinking about important information and main ideas, monitor their understanding, summarize and synthesize in real time as they are reading, and later discuss with peers (Fisher and Frey 2014). Students annotate by "coding" text using markings or symbols to represent new information, points of confusion, connection, and so on. Students highlight unknown words, important facts, and questions they have. For narrative text, students can find and annotate evidence of character traits or the theme, problem, or solution. In informational text, annotations can be made to track main ideas and key details or to make connections between visuals and diagrams and the body of the text.

Materials
- *Annotate and Compare* (page 86)
- text selection
- sticky notes

Process
1. Prepare by selecting a piece of text for students to annotate. The text should provide multiple opportunities for students to practice the various annotation symbols.
2. Explain that annotation involves making notes directly on a text, in the margins or by underlining or highlighting key information. Sticky notes can be used to annotate a nonconsumable text. Show students the basic annotations (see page 86).
3. Conduct a think-aloud and model how to read a portion of the text and use annotation symbols to mark your thinking.
4. Provide students with the *Annotate and Compare* activity sheet. Distribute sticky notes if you are using nonconsumable texts. Have students read a portion of the text and annotate it.

5. Give students time to share their annotations with partners. Encourage them to explain their annotations to one another and compare and contrast the similarities and differences in what they annotated. They can note these comparisons on the activity sheet.

6. Have a class discussion asking students to share their annotations and thinking. Clarify misunderstandings or misapplication of annotation if necessary.

Differentiation

Scaffold the lesson by introducing the annotations one at a time and providing a series of lessons focused on each annotation symbol. Some students may benefit from hearing the reading selection read aloud as they follow along and make annotations. Encourage students with advanced skills to personalize and extend their annotation key, adding symbols they think will be useful when reading.

Name: _____   Date: _____

Annotate and Compare

Directions: As you read, use the symbols to monitor your thinking. After reading, work with a partner to compare the symbols you both used.

Annotation	When to Use It
___	Underline important information, main points
○	Circle key words, phrases, or points of confusion
?	Questions you have (be sure to write your question)
!	Something that caught your attention or surprised you

Comparing with My Partner

One annotation my partner and I both made:

_____

_____

_____

One annotation that was different:

_____

_____

_____

One annotation I added to my text after discussing with my partner:

_____

_____

_____

Structured Annotation

Objectives

- Read closely to determine what the text says explicitly and to make logical inferences from it; cite specific textual evidence when writing or speaking to support conclusions drawn from the text.

Background Information

Structured Annotation is a strategy that helps students connect to, stay engaged with, and better understand text. Structured Annotation emphasizes key ideas by providing students with a narrow focus. The teacher provides specific prompts, and students annotate by "coding" text using markings or symbols. For narrative text, students can find and annotate evidence of character traits or the theme, problem, or solution. In informational text, annotations can be made to track main ideas and key details or to make connections between visuals and diagrams and the body of the text.

Materials

- text selection and prompts based on it
- sticky notes

Process

1. Review the text and develop prompts that focus on key points students will identify. For example, you may wish to have students focus on a specific character, details about the character, the impact of the character's actions, and so on. Write annotation prompts accordingly.

2. Explain that annotating involves marking text for a specific purpose. Making annotations supports comprehension by helping readers focus and keep track of important information and key points in a text.

3. Provide the prompts and discuss the specific annotations students will use, such as the following.
   - Circle words that tell the problem the character is trying to solve.
   - Underline details that show how the character tried to solve the problem.
   - Put a box around the effects of the character's actions.

4. Assign students a text and give them time to read and respond to the prompts. After students annotate the text, have them share with partners, explaining their thinking and the significance of the annotations.

5. Have a class discussion and ask students to share their thinking about the text and annotations. Clarify misunderstandings as needed.

Differentiation

Some students may benefit from hearing the text selection read aloud as they follow along and make annotations. Scaffold the process by having students work with partners to annotate the text. Challenge students with advanced reading skills to develop their own additional prompts with unique markings.

Line-by-Line Reading

Objectives
- Read closely to determine what the text says explicitly and to make logical inferences from it; cite specific textual evidence when writing or speaking to support conclusions drawn from the text.

Background Information
Line-by-Line Reading (Lemov, Driggs, and Woolway 2016) is a close reading strategy that supports comprehension and the development of critical thinking skills. Reading closely requires readers to comprehend the author's purpose, make connections, and construct and reconstruct meaning as they read and reread text (Fisher and Frey 2012). Line-by-Line Reading helps students unpack and analyze chunks of text methodically before proceeding. Adolescent readers will benefit from using close reading strategies such as Line-by-Line Reading as they encounter challenging texts.

Materials
- text selection

Process
1. Prepare for the lesson by selecting a text worthy of a close reading. The text should include complex ideas students can explore and discuss and should be one students will want to reread to learn more and think deeper about the author's writing and message.
2. Preview the text in advance and note where you will have students stop to discuss the text. This depends on the text and the complexity of the ideas, but it could be every two or three sentences, for example.
3. Give students time to read the first short segment of text. After reading, help students identify the key ideas in the text using questions such as these:
   - What ideas is the author presenting?
   - What important words does the author use?
   - What facts, evidence, or other items of significance, such as events, are presented?
4. After discussing the meaning of the text, move on to the next section and repeat the process. Have students read the section and then discuss it as a class.

5. When appropriate, revisit the sections read previously to discuss how the author builds meaning.

6. When finished reading and analyzing the text, summarize the process and what was learned through the line-by-line reading.

Differentiation

Students may benefit by working in small groups to analyze a text with teacher support. Students who are ready can work with partners to read and analyze text segments at their own pace.

GRASP

Objectives

- Determine two or more central ideas in a text and analyze their development over the course of the text; provide an objective summary of the text.

Background Information

Summarizing is a skill that is difficult for students to learn (Duke and Pearson 2002), but it offers tremendous benefits. Summarizing improves readers' abilities to locate main ideas and supporting details, identify and omit unnecessary details and redundant material, remember what is read, analyze text structure and see how ideas are related, generalize details, clarify meaning, take notes, and rethink what they have read so that they can process it more deeply. GRASP teaches students to independently summarize to understand and learn material they are reading (Hayes 1989). The strategy increases students' abilities to recall information, self-correct, organize materials, and read informational texts proficiently. The strength of this strategy is the step-by-step scaffolding of summary writing, a skill that will support students' content learning now and in the future.

Materials

- *GRASP* (page 94)
- text selection

Process

1. Tell students that they are going to be learning how to summarize what they have read. Explain that summarizing is a useful tool that can help them understand, remember, and think about what they read so that they can learn it more deeply.

2. Direct students to read a section of the text with the purpose of trying to remember all they can. After they have finished reading, ask them to tell you what they remember.

3. List what students remember and then have them reread the selection to see if there is any other information that should be included on the list and to confirm the list is correct. Any incorrect information should be corrected.

4. Evaluate the list as a class to identify the main idea or ideas of the passage. Group the information on the list accordingly.

5. Using the organizational structure created by categorizing the information, work with the class and model how to write a short summary of the material in one category. Show students how to omit unnecessary information, combine as much information as possible, and add information to make the summary read naturally and coherently.

6. Continue for the other categories, modeling the process in detail. When students have learned the process, have them use the *GRASP* activity sheet to help them construct their summaries independently.

Differentiation

Students who need support should have the text available to them during the "Details Remembered from Reading" stage of the activity. Some students may benefit from having the teacher read the selection aloud, rephrasing sections and providing explanations. This activity can be further differentiated by allowing students to work with partners or in small groups to remember the information and construct the summary. Students who are ready can be encouraged to work independently.

GRASP Example

Details Remembered from Text

Matter is anything that takes up space.

Matter has physical properties.

Shape, size, temperature, feel, smell, and taste are all physical properties.

Matter can have color or be clear.

Matter can be big or small.

Matter can be hot or cold.

Matter can be rough or smooth.

The wind is matter.

Matter can taste sweet, sour, salty, and bitter.

Smells can be strong or faint.

Matter can bend, bounce, stretch, or break.

Matter can be liquid, gas, or solid.

Additions/Corrections

Use your senses to observe physical properties.

Solids don't lose their shape.

Liquid takes the shape of its container.

Gas does not have a shape.

Main Ideas in Text

Matter has many physical properties.

The physical properties are observed by our senses—see, hear, feel, taste, and smell.

Matter has different states: solids, liquids, or gases.

Name: _____ Date:_____

GRASP

Directions: After reading a text, write details you remember. Reread the text and write additional information. Review the lists and identify the main ideas and details. Write a summary of the main ideas.

Details Remembered from Text	Additions/Corrections

Main Ideas in Text

Thinking at Right Angles

Objectives

- Read closely to determine what the text says explicitly and to make logical inferences from it; cite specific textual evidence when writing or speaking to support conclusions drawn from the text.

Background Information

Thinking at Right Angles (Tileston 2006) is a close reading strategy that supports comprehension and the development of critical thinking skills. Reading closely requires readers to comprehend the author's purpose, make connections, and construct and reconstruct meaning as they read, reread, and annotate text (Fisher and Frey 2012). This strategy is useful in helping students consider textual evidence when composing responses to texts—an essential skill for reading and writing in grades 6–12 (Gormley and McDermott 2015). After an initial quick read of a text, readers return for a closer reading for evidence or facts in the text. They think about the evidence or facts, make personal connections, and compose a summary, bringing together the textual evidence and their feelings about it. Adolescent readers and writers will benefit from repeated practice with close reading strategies such as Thinking at Right Angles.

Materials

- *Thinking at Right Angles* (page 98)
- text selection

Process

1. Prepare for the lesson by selecting a text worthy of a close reading. The text should include complex ideas students can explore, discuss, and write about and should be one students will want to reread to learn more and think deeper about the author's writing and message.
2. Provide time for students to complete an initial reading of the text.
3. Explain to students they will reread the text, reading closely for facts, evidence, or other items of significance in the text, such as events. Distribute copies of *Thinking in Right Angles*.
4. Allow students time to complete the close reading of the text, recording their facts and evidence on their activity sheets.

5. Prompt students to think about the text evidence they collected and identify feelings or personal connections they may have to the text. Have students write their responses on their activity sheets.

6. Have students compose summaries that bring together points from the textual evidence and their personal connections. After they finish writing the summaries, have students share their understanding and thinking with partners.

Differentiation

Younger adolescent readers may need more scaffolding to use this strategy. Scaffolds might include selecting the evidence and/or facts as a whole class and then allowing time for students to individually make connections and write summaries. In addition, students may need more support in bringing the evidence together in the summary. This can be accomplished through thinking aloud and providing model summaries. Students with advanced reading skills can extend the connections they make into questions for inquiry and then find answers to their questions.

Thinking at Right Angles *Example*

Title of text: Game Changers: Lin-Manuel Miranda

Step 1: Facts/Evidence

Lin-Manuel Miranda spoke Spanish at home but English at school.

Grew up in a mostly Hispanic neighborhood of Manhattan

Listened to salsa at home, rap at school and with friends

Visited Puerto Rico every summer with his parents

"You change identities when you go home and any time you can try a different identity that's helpful in being a writer or performer." p. 8

Step 2: Feelings/Connections

Having to learn how to be in two different cultures when growing up can be valuable for kids. Sometimes it might make you feel disconnected, like I used to sometimes be embarrassed at school about the lunches my mom made because everyone else was just eating sandwiches, but now I am older and I think it is good I know about different foods and speak another language and know other traditions.

Step 3: Summary

Being bicultural is an asset. Kids can learn valuable skills when they have to bridge one culture at home and one culture at school. It can make them successful in life. Lin-Manuel Miranda is a great example of this. Growing up his parents raised him with a strong Latino identity. They spoke Spanish at home, and he lived in a mostly Hispanic neighborhood. They went back and visited Puerto Rico every summer. This was very different from school where he only spoke and learned in English and was around other types of students. In the text *Game Changers: Lin-Manuel Miranda,* he talks about the role his bicultural identity plays in his successful career as a playwriter and an actor. On page 8, he tells the reader, "You change identities when you go home and any time you can try a different identity that's helpful in being a writer or performer." He believes it helped make him successful.

Name: _____ Date:_____

Thinking at Right Angles

Directions: Write evidence or facts that are important to the meaning of the text. Think about connections you have to this evidence. Write a summary that explains the connections using the textual evidence.

Title of text: _____

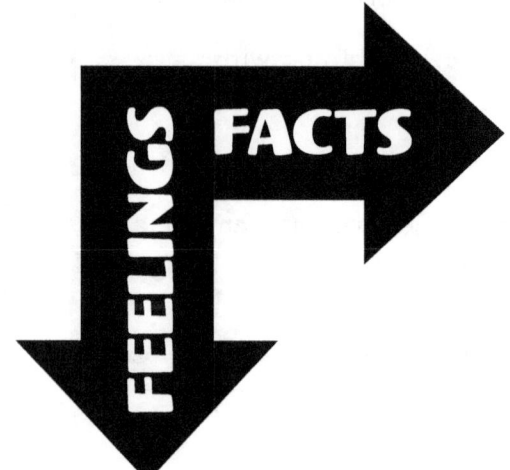

Step 1: Facts/Evidence

Step 2: Feelings/Connections

Step 3: Summary

98 Literacy Strategies—131699 © Shell Education

Question Journal

Objectives

- Refer to details and examples in a text when explaining what the text says explicitly and when drawing inferences from the text.
- Determine the main idea of a text and explain how it is supported by key details; summarize the text.

Background Information

Question Journals are an informal but effective way to help students identify key details in an informational text. Students keep question journals throughout the year and use them to answer questions they are asked and to generate questions of their own. This strategy gradually releases the responsibility of monitoring comprehension through questioning from teachers to students, moving students toward independence. Students generate questions before, during, and after reading, which reinforces skills such as setting a purpose, monitoring and clarifying, and being an active reader. Note that students are likely to rely on asking "Right There" and "Think and Search" questions since those are explicit and easy to generate; therefore you may want to provide extensive modeling of "Author and Me" questions.

Materials

- *Question Journal* (page 102)
- text selection
- sticky notes

Process

1. Prepare for the lesson by selecting a complex informational text. Segment the text into several sections that students will read silently. This should be done for the whole-class lesson, and also for subsequent lessons when students will be working independently with partners or small groups. Post the section start and stop points for student reference, or have students mark the sections in the text if appropriate. Have students use sticky notes to mark the end of a section and to record their questions in their notebooks or on the *Question Journal* activity sheet.

2. Tell students to think of questions they should ask before they read the text. Allow time for students to generate a question on their own or in pairs. Have students share some of the questions they came up with. Lead a discussion to identify the type of each question. Have students generate and record possible answers to their questions.

3. Give students time to read and then allow them to answer their questions, citing evidence from the text. If needed, model giving complete responses to their questions, providing details and text evidence. Explain that "I don't know" is not an acceptable response to a question. If a poor or unanswerable question is asked, model how to think about the question, rephrase, or query the question-asker for clarification.

4. Prepare the students to read the next segment of text. Provide a question for them to consider while they read this section and encourage them to generate a question of their own. Model asking "Author and Me" questions if appropriate.

5. Assess student readiness to work on the remainder of the text in partners or small groups. The whole class or specific students may need more teacher modeling or support before working independently. Encourage students who are ready to work independently to monitor the questions they ask and answer by using sticky notes or the *Question Journal* activity sheet. Circulate among groups while they work independently to ensure students are challenging one another to think deeply about the text.

Differentiation

This is a flexible strategy that can be used for whole-class and small-group instruction. Students who need extra support generating questions from the text may find it useful to use the *Question Journal* activity sheet. This resource encourages students to think of a variety of questions while they read and scaffolds ways to think about the questions they are asked by their partners or groupmates. Challenge students by having them research questions that were unanswered by the text.

Types of Questions	
In the Text	**In My Head**
Right There The answer to the question can be found easily and immediately in the text. The words used to create the question are the same words used in the text.	**Author and Me** The answer to the question is not found directly in the text. The reader has to think about the information that the author provided, prior knowledge about the topic, and personal experience. The reader has to make connections to answer the question.
Think and Search The answer to the question can be found in the text, but the reader may have to combine two parts of the text to arrive at an answer. The words in the question may not directly lead the reader to the answer in the text. The reader has to make connections to arrive at an answer.	

Question Journal *Example*

Types of Questions		
Right There	Think and Search	Author and Me

Questions and Answers

Before Reading Questions	Possible Answers	Answers/Evidence
What is Taino? (Right There) Did the three ships stay together? (Right There) What made the journey difficult? (Right There) Why did Columbus want to find a way to Asia? (Right There)	It might be a place Columbus found. I can't imagine they did. I think it would be hard and probably scary and a long trip. He wanted to find a shorter way there.	Taino are the native people of the Caribbean (p. 4). All 3 ships made it to the islands, but one finally had to be abandoned (p. 7). There was almost a mutiny, and the food was rotten (p. 6). He wanted to find a trade route to Asia that was shorter (p. 4).
During Reading Questions	Possible Answers	Answers/Evidence
Why did Ferdinand and Isabella fund the expedition? (Think and Search) Why did Columbus think he landed on the coast of Asia? (Think and Search or Right There)	They probably wanted to get rich and to get fancy things like gold and spices and jewels from Asia. Maybe he had never been to Asia and didn't know what it looked like?	They wanted to have an advantage over Portugal in trading to make Spain richer (p. 5). He didn't know there was land between Europe and Asia, he thought Asia was across from Europe (p. 8).
After Reading Questions	Possible Answers	Answers/Evidence
How did Columbus change the lives of the Taino? (Author and Me) What did Ferdinand and Isabella get from the expedition? (Think and Search)	He probably made them slaves and maybe they died from diseases like I learned in 4th grade about the Indigenous Americans.	The Taino were made slaves and many of them died, he ruined their culture (p. 9). It doesn't really tell us.

Name: _____ Date:_____

Question Journal

Directions: Record your questions before and during reading. Label the type of each question. As you read and discuss, write the answers and more questions. After reading, write questions you still have.

Types of Questions		
Right There	Think and Search	Author and Me

Questions and Answers

Before Reading Questions	Possible Answers	Answers/Evidence
During Reading Questions	Possible Answers	Answers/Evidence
After Reading Questions	Possible Answers	Answers/Evidence

COMPREHENSION: STRATEGIES

Facts-Questions-Responses (FQR)

Objectives

- Determine the central ideas or information from a primary or secondary source; provide an accurate summary of the source distinct from prior knowledge or opinions.

Background Information

As students engage with increased volume and complexity of text in the secondary grades, they need to be able to organize and make sense of names, dates, processes, procedures, and other statements of fact to build their content knowledge. Facts-Questions-Responses (Harvey and Goudvis 2017) is a note-taking and reading comprehension strategy to help students understand and remember facts and information they read. Learning to take good notes is a valuable academic skill for students in grades 6–12. As students read independently, they note key ideas, generate questions, and respond to their facts, questions, or both. This strategy may need intensive modeling at first before gradually releasing responsibility to students. It is best taught as a whole- or small-group teacher-directed lesson several times. Students should work toward using this strategy independently while they read and then use their notes as the basis of class discussion.

Materials

- *Facts-Questions-Responses* (page 106)
- text selection

Process

1. Introduce the text selection and review the *Facts-Questions-Responses* activity sheet with students.
2. Model reading the first paragraph and using *Facts-Questions-Responses* to take notes. The process is as follows:
   a. Students take notes on key ideas they consider to be facts.
   b. Students generate questions they have about the facts. The questions often reflect students making connections, attempting to clarify misunderstandings or fill gaps in their knowledge, or setting a purpose for future learning about the topic.
   c. They then respond to their facts, questions, or both. Here students provide personal reactions to the text as they explain their thinking and understanding, and make inferences and connections.

3. Conduct a think-aloud to model your thought processes while note-taking, explaining which facts you think are important or interesting. Model writing a question in response to the facts you recorded.

4. Direct students to read the selection, or a segment of the selection, and record facts from the selection and questions they may have.

5. Conduct a class discussion of the facts students gleaned and the questions students generated. Model responses to the facts and questions through a think-aloud.

6. Continue this process to read the remainder of the text selection.

7. Questions students generate are often answered later in the text or during class discussions. If interesting and relevant questions remain unanswered, have students use the internet or other resources to find the answers.

8. As students become more familiar with FQR, gradually release responsibility by having students shift from working as a whole class to working in small groups or with partners to independent reading and note-taking. Conclude with whole-class discussions.

Differentiation

Some students may benefit from using sticky notes to annotate or code the text. After reading, they can engage in a discussion with the teacher or partners to be sure they have accurately labeled information as facts. Then they record the facts on their activity sheets. Additionally, providing question stems or sentence starters as scaffolds for the Questions and Responses columns may be helpful. FQR can also be used as a listening comprehension activity or while viewing video resources.

Sentence Stems		
Facts	**Questions**	**Responses**
I read	I wonder	I think
I noticed	Who?	I understand
The text said	What?	I question
I learned	Where?	I feel
I remember	When?	I believe
	Why?	
	How?	

Facts-Questions-Responses Example

Facts	Questions	Responses
Africa is the second-largest continent.	Which is the largest continent?	Asia!
Trading made African cultures rich. If they lost control of trade routes, they lost power and wealth.	How would African kingdoms lose control of trade routes?	Ivory, weapons, gold, salt, and different crops were all traded on the African trade routes—control of the routes could be gained or lost during wars/fights with other groups.
The Kush were rich because they controlled important routes to Egypt.	What kind of things were being traded?	

Name: _____ Date: _____

Facts-Questions-Responses

Directions: Record interesting or useful facts you learn. Write questions that occur to you. Write your responses to the facts or questions.

Title: _____

Facts	Questions	Responses

Get the GIST

Objectives

- Cite textual evidence that most strongly supports an analysis of what the text says explicitly as well as inferences drawn from the text.
- Determine a central idea of a text and analyze its development over the course of the text, including its relationship to supporting ideas; provide an objective summary of the text.

Background Information

Get the GIST is a content-area reading strategy adapted from the GIST (Generating Interactions between Schemata and Text) strategy (Cunningham 1982; Moore et al. 2002). Get the GIST asks students to explain the "gist" of the text by taking notes as they read, writing short summary statements, and then combining these statements to write a concise summary of the text. This process chunks the reading of content-area text, encourages students to monitor their comprehension and integrate important information, and helps students remember the most important key details and concepts from the reading. As with other summarizing activities, Get the GIST encourages students to focus on the most important information, eliminate extraneous details, and explain the material or topic in their own words. The end goal is to write a one-paragraph summary of about three to four sentences.

Materials

- *Get the Gist* (page 110)
- text selection

Process

1. Prepare for the lesson by previewing the text students will read and determining appropriate stopping points where students can pause to take notes on the reading and monitor their comprehension. If possible, choose a section of text that is no more than three to four paragraphs long or one that addresses an important concept or topic.
2. Introduce the strategy to students by explaining that as they read independently, they will pay attention to and take notes on the important ideas in the passage. Distribute copies of *Get the GIST*.

3. Explain the three steps students can use to guide their note-taking and write their short summary statements:

   a. Write "who" or "what" this section is about.

   b. Think about and write the most important information about the "who" or "what."

   c. In your own words, write a GIST (main idea) statement that combines the information from steps a and b.

   When explaining steps a and b, discuss ways to locate main ideas and the most important information in text, such as locating the topic sentence of each paragraph, or looking for key words and phrases. When explaining step c, discuss the characteristics and qualities of a good summary.

4. Model using the *Get the GIST* activity sheet with the first section of the text students will read. Be sure to think aloud as you attend to the important information students should pay attention to when they read. Model how to record notes on the activity sheet and how to write a short summary statement.

5. Allow students time to read the remaining chunks of text and record their notes. When students are finished reading, have a class or partner discussion about the notes they recorded and have students share their summary statements.

6. Direct students to combine their summary statements into a short summary paragraph that explains the GIST of the text. Explain that the paragraph should be about three to four sentences long, include only the most important details, and present information in the order it was presented in the text. Students can use revision techniques if their summaries are longer. Have students share their summary paragraphs with partners or small groups.

Differentiation

When introducing this strategy, students may require additional modeling for both note-taking and writing the summary paragraph. Scaffold students' use of this strategy by completing the reading one section at a time and discussing it as a class in between each section. Students may benefit from working with partners, stopping to discuss between sections to be sure they each understood the section and writing the short summary statement together. Students who have advanced understanding of the content or strong summarization skills can work independently on GIST or move directly to writing summary paragraphs after reading rather than chunking the text.

Get the GIST Example

Section	Who or what is this section about?	What is important about "who" or "what"?	GIST statement
1. page 34	echinoderms like sea stars	invertebrates marine animals have a hard spiny skin radial symmetry multiple arms (5 or more)	Echinoderms are marine animals with a hard spiny skin and multiple arms.
2. page 34	echinoderms nervous system	simple nervous system, no brains simple eye-light and dark only	Echinoderms have multiple arms and simple nervous systems.
3. page 35	echinoderms reproductive system	either male or female 100 million eggs at once can also regrow if an arm breaks off (asexual reproduction)	Echinoderms can reproduce sexually or asexually.

Combine your GIST statements in a three- to four-sentence summary paragraph.

Echinoderms, like sea stars, are marine animals that have a hard, spiny skin and multiple arms. They have a simple nervous system with no brain and an eye that can see only light and dark. They can reproduce sexually, using eggs and sperm from the male and female, or asexually by growing from a broken arm of an adult.

Name: _____ Date:_____

Get the GIST

Directions: Read each section of the text. Take notes and answer the questions. Write a GIST (main idea) statement for each section. Write a summary paragraph that explains the GIST of the text.

Section	Who or what is this section about?	What is important about "who" or "what"?	GIST statement

Combine your GIST statements in a three- to four-sentence summary paragraph.

_____
_____
_____
_____
_____
_____
_____

Activity sheet adapted from the "Get the GIST Log for Students" by the Middle School Matters Institute.

Double Entry Journal

Objectives

- Determine the central ideas or conclusions of a text; provide an accurate summary of the text distinct from prior knowledge or opinions.

Background Information

Double Entry Journals are reader response journals in which students quote from a text and then respond to it. The Double Entry Journal is a valuable tool to build content knowledge and promote engagement with text (Blachowicz and Ogle 2001). Because this strategy connects reading and writing, secondary students are likely to benefit from enhanced comprehension of the reading material. Students can use a Double Entry Journal to help them understand and respond to text in a variety of ways. These journals can be used across content areas to study concepts or vocabulary, express and justify opinions, and analyze text. Double Entry Journals can also be used for reading and researching online.

Materials

- *Double Entry Journal* (page 114)
- text selection

Process

1. Distribute copies of the *Double Entry Journal* activity sheet or have students fold sheets of notebook paper in half lengthwise to create two columns.

2. Share with students that they will be reading a text selection independently and recording information from the text as they read. Explain that in the left column, they can quote passages, sentences, phrases, vocabulary terms, or anything from the text they believe is relevant to understanding and thinking about the meaning of the text. They may also record things they find confusing or challenging.

3. Explain that in the right column, students can respond to and reflect on the text they recorded, expressing their thoughts, reactions, insights, and inferences in relation to the text. They can make note of questions the text raises, explanations or clarifications of concepts and terminology, connections to their own beliefs or values, or how the text makes them feel.

4. Model by conducting a think-aloud that demonstrates how to select meaningful material from the text. Explain your reasoning for selecting the quote, passage, or word, and model how to write an appropriate reflection in the right column.

5. Direct students to read the text independently using their Double Entry Journals to record and reflect on their reading.

6. Have students engage in a class, group, or partner discussion to share what they wrote in their journals.

Differentiation

Students may benefit from additional modeling when the strategy is introduced, the text is challenging, or the topic of the text is unfamiliar. Scaffold journal use by providing parameters for selecting passages and quotes. For example, you may direct students to only make note of a particular concept such as author's craft or references to the role of women in a historical piece. This can focus students' attention toward a specific lesson objective and/or build their skills for using Double Entry Journals more independently in the future.

Double Entry Journal *Example*

Title: To Kill a Mockingbird

Quotes/Ideas from Text	My Thoughts and Ideas
"There's some folks who don't eat like us," she whispered fiercely, "but you ain't called onto contradict 'em at the table when they don't. That boy's yo' comp'ny and if he wants to eat up the table cloth you let him, you hear?" (p.32) "He was the filthiest human I had ever seen. His neck was dark grey, the backs of his hands were rusty, and his fingernails were black deep into the quick." (p.35)	I think Calpurnia is trying to teach Scout to be respectful of differences in people when she tells her to "not contradict 'em." She doesn't want her to make Walter feel bad that he is eating so much syrup, but maybe she also wants Scout to understand that people are different and there are reasons for being different they can't help or that it's not bad to be different, like maybe he's eating all that syrup because they don't have a lot at their house if they are poorer than the Finches. I wonder if the author wants you to be disgusted by Burris because this description makes me feel that way. Maybe she wants us to hate Burris, or maybe we are supposed to feel sorry for him. I don't know yet.

Title: Beginnings of the War

Quotes/Ideas from Text	My Thoughts and Ideas
April 19, 1775 "the shot heard 'round the world" British casualties: 273; 73 Killed, 174 wounded, 26 missing. Colonial casualties: 96; 49 killed, 41 wounded, and 5 missing.	I didn't realize the Battles of Lexington and Concord started the war in April 1775!! It's earlier than I thought. I think this is a famous quote because it was the first time that a colony was going to go against a King, and so everyone was paying attention to what was going to happen next. I wonder what missing means? Did the soldiers run away and they never found them after the battle?

Name: _____ Date: _____

Double Entry Journal

Directions: As you read, record quotes, ideas, words, or other information from the text. Write your thoughts about the material from the text.

Title: _____

Quotes/Ideas from Text	My Thoughts and Ideas

Reciprocal Teaching

Objectives

- Read and comprehend complex literary and informational texts independently and proficiently.

Background Information

Reciprocal Teaching (Palinscar and Brown 1984) is a collaborative strategy in which students work together in small groups, practicing and applying four reading comprehension strategies to co-construct the meaning of text. This strategy encourages metacognition and active reading, both characteristics of skilled reading. Reciprocal Teaching is a highly effective yet infrequently used strategy (Hattie 2009; Fisher and Frey 2018). Students in grades 6–12 should be familiar with the four comprehension strategies used during reciprocal teaching—summarizing, questioning, clarifying, and predicting—but may require a review during the initial lesson(s). This strategy is intended to release responsibility for learning to students as they practice and internalize these strategies. It may take multiple repeated lessons using Reciprocal Teaching for students to transition to full ownership of the strategies and for the process to become completely student-led (Fisher and Frey 2018).

Materials

- *Reciprocal Teaching Notes* (page 117)
- *Reciprocal Teaching Role Cards* (page 118)
- text selection

Process

1. Select a text and decide where it should be segmented based on the lexical complexity of the text and the complexity of the content. Each segment should be long enough to allow students to apply reading strategies, but not so long that multiple key concepts (informational text) or multiple key events (literary text) occur in the segment.

2. Determine student groups. Research demonstrates this strategy is highly effective and benefits readers across all levels; however, it may be useful to create groups of students with varying reading skills.

3. Review and model the reading strategies (summarizing, questioning, clarifying, and predicting), explaining what they are and how they are used. Select two or more combinations of the four strategies and use direct instruction with students. Model

how to use the strategies by providing examples and conducting think-alouds during the reading to demonstrate how to use the strategies in conjunction with one another. Guide readers as they apply and practice the strategies together while reading a selection of the text. This step may require successive lessons.

4. After practicing the strategies, place students in groups of four and assign (or have them self-assign) a role for each member: summarizer, questioner, clarifier, or predictor. The *Reciprocal Teaching Role Cards* may be a useful tool for students.

5. Distribute *Reciprocal Teaching Notes* and direct students to read the first segment of the text silently. Encourage students to annotate or code the text as they read and take notes for their role on the activity sheet.

6. Students then discuss the text in their groups, sharing information based on their assigned roles.
   - The summarizer highlights key ideas from the text segment.
   - The questioner poses literal and higher-order questions.
   - The clarifier addresses parts of the text that may be unclear, helps make connections, clarifies contradicted predictions, or addresses some of the higher-order questions asked.
   - The predictor makes predictions about what will happen next or predicts how the learning connects to previous knowledge.

7. Students switch roles and read the next segment of the text, repeating the process. They continue the process until they complete the reading assignment.

Differentiation

Students may benefit from having access to the *Reciprocal Teaching Role Cards* with sentence stems and question-starters to be used during discussions. Readers who need more support will benefit from shorter segments of text. Advanced readers can be directed to read ahead, or combine multiple strategies while reading each segment.

Name: _____ Date:_____

Reciprocal Teaching Notes

Directions: As you read, complete the information for your role. As you listen and discuss after reading, take notes for the other roles.

Text: _____

Summarizer: What are the big ideas in the text? What important information should we know?	**Questioner:** Pose questions about what is happening in the text.
Clarifier: Were there any points of confusion in the text? Words that were confusing? Did you use any fix-up strategies?	**Predictor:** Make predictions or draw inferences about what will happen in the text.

Name: _____ Date: _____

Reciprocal Teaching Role Cards

Summarizer

Summaries are main ideas and key details that tell us what the text was about. When we summarize, we leave out information that is not essential.

Useful Summarizing Strategies

- Look at the first and last sentence of each paragraph.
- Ask and answer: Who? What? Where? When? Why?
- Look for key words.
- Annotate as you read.
- Try and explain the "gist" of the text.

Predictor

Predictions are good guesses about what you think you will learn or what will happen in the text. Good readers make predictions before and during reading.

Useful Prediction Tools

- Look at headings, pictures, charts, and diagrams.
- Make connections to what you already know.
- Skim, scan, and reread.

Prediction Starters

Based on (a clue), I think ____.

Based on what I already know about ____, I think that ____.

Questioner

Good readers ask questions about the text as they read. This helps you deepen your understanding of what happens in the text and make connections to things you already know or have learned.

Question Ideas

- What is happening?
- When is ____?
- Who is ____?
- Where is ____?
- Why is ____ important?
- What does ____?
- What might ____?
- Why does ____?
- How are ____ and ____ alike/different?
- Why do you think ____?

Clarifier

Good readers notice when they do not understand something in the text or when they come to a confusing point or word in the reading.

Signs You Might Need to Clarify

- You can't remember what you just read.
- You lose your place in the text.
- You are not sure what a word means.
- There is a confusing part you have to reread.
- There is a complicated part of the text.

Tools for Clarifying

- Reread the section or read ahead.
- Check pictures, diagrams, or headings for clues.
- Look up a word or use word-learning strategies.

Text Rendering

Objectives

- Engage in a range of collaborative discussions with diverse partners on grade-level topics, texts, and issues, building on others' ideas and expressing their own clearly.

Background Information

Text Rendering (Davis-Haley 2004; Fisher and Frey 2020) is a text-based discussion strategy that can be used to read and discuss any type of text. Students work together to construct meaning, clarify, and expand thinking about text. Discussion-based instruction is a vital part of effective comprehension instruction in grades 6–12. While many teachers require discussion in secondary classrooms, there is often a lack of structure or explicit instruction on how to have productive text-based discussion. Text Rendering is a useful strategy because it scaffolds and provides students a specific purpose for a discussion. Students are more likely to participate and have meaningful discussions if they understand the purpose and the construct of the discussion (Stengel-Eskin et al. 2019). Text Rendering works well for close reading or rereading a text.

Materials

- *Text Rendering* (page 122)
- text selection

Process

1. Prepare for the lesson by selecting text for the discussion. This can be any type of text in any content area. Have students read the text prior to the discussion.

2. Introduce the discussion by explaining to students that they will work together in small groups to have a discussion that helps them better understand the main idea of the text and learn from one another.

3. Place students in groups of four or five. Provide each student with a *Text Rendering* activity sheet. Alternately, provide each group with one activity sheet or sheet of chart paper and have the group select a scribe to record the information from the discussion.

4. Provide time for students to individually review the text. Direct them to identify from the text one sentence, one phrase, and one word they feel is significant. Remind them it is okay if other students share the same sentence, phrase, or word. That likely means they have indeed found something of significance in the text.

5. Facilitate a discussion in three rounds:
   - First Round: Each group member shares the sentence they selected.
   - Second Round: Each group member shares the phrase they selected.
   - Third Round: Each group member shares the word they selected.

   Students record what members of their group share on the *Text Rendering* activity sheet, or the scribe records the information for the group.

6. Group members then discuss what they heard and what the text says. Provide general discussion prompts or have students use the prompts on the activity sheet.

7. Debrief as a whole class so students can gain insight into the multiple perspectives of classmates.

Differentiation

Students may benefit from participating in Text Rendering as a whole class the first few times it is used. Rather than each member sharing all three pieces of text (sentence, phrase, or word), have students share one piece, and lead students in a whole-class discussion. This may help those who are initially reluctant to share and supports students when the text is particularly challenging. Students who demonstrate proficiency with Text Rendering or who are comfortable tackling it on their own may work in small independent groups.

Text Rendering *Example*

Text: The Raven

> A significant **sentence:** "In there stepped a Raven of the saintly days of yore"

What group members said:

- As of someone gently rapping, rapping at my chamber door
- Same as mine
- And the Raven, never flitting, still is sitting, still is sitting

> A significant **phrase:** "nothing more"

What group members said:

- Nothing more
- Nothing more
- Nothing more—we all picked nothing more!

> A significant **word:** Raven

What group members said:

- Lenore—probably the name of an important friend or person
- Lenore—his girlfriend or wife, maybe they died
- Raven

Name: _____   Date: _____

Text Rendering

Directions: Choose one sentence, one phrase, and one word you think are significant to understanding the meaning of the text. Write them in the boxes. Record the contributions of your group members.

Text:

A significant **sentence**:

What group members said:

- _____
- _____
- _____

A significant **phrase**:

What group members said:

- _____
- _____
- _____

A significant **word**:

What group members said:

- _____
- _____
- _____

Discussion Prompts:
- What new insights have you gained about the text by looking at it in this way?
- What do you think this text is essentially about?
- What do some of the phrases or words seem to imply about the text? Is this similar or different to the overall meaning?

SECTION III:
Writing

The strategies in this section correspond with key competencies identified in *What the Science of Reading Says about Writing* (Jump and Wolfe 2023). These research-based instructional strategies will help teachers bridge the gap between the science of literacy instruction and classroom practice.

Strategy	Skills and Understandings Addressed				
	Genre Characteristics	Prewriting and Organization	Revise for Purpose	Grammar, Usage, and Mechanics	Responding to Reading
Genre Analysis	■				
EASE (Examine, Assess, Suggest, Envision)	■				
RAFT	■				
Expository Writing Frames	■				
Scholarly Texts	■				
Planning for Writing		■			

Strategy	Skills and Understandings Addressed *(cont.)*				
	Genre Characteristics	Prewriting and Organization	Revise for Purpose	Grammar, Usage, and Mechanics	Responding to Reading
Composing a Draft		■			
R.A.C.E. Organizer		■			
Revising Writing			■		
Editing Writing				■	
Reading Response					■
Read, Reread, List, Compose (RRLC)					■

Writing

The connection between reading and writing is complex and intricate, placing the act of reading as a necessary and crucial counterpart to writing. This reading-writing connection is obvious to most educators, yet reading and writing have traditionally been taught as separate subjects (Dewitz et al. 2020), and commonly reading instruction takes precedence over writing. Teachers can face many obstacles when it comes to teaching writing: writing well and teaching it well takes time and focus. In some states, standardized testing emphasizes reading and writing despite the lack of an explicit focus on writing in the curriculum. Additional obstacles include students' reading abilities, which can hamper their writing abilities and their motivation for writing. Increasingly, however, educators are embracing a combined approach to reading and writing instruction as they recognize the benefits of doing so (Dewitz et al. 2020; Graham and Hebert 2010). Teachers recognize that given the complex communication realities of the modern world, the ability to write well across a variety of mediums and genres is critical to academic and career success. They also acknowledge that reading and writing are reciprocal processes. Reading and reading instruction can improve the organization and quality of writing. Writing instruction can improve reading fluency and comprehension.

> Emphasizing writing in all content areas enhances learning and develops critical thinking skills. Students are more likely to retain information they read when they write about it (Graham and Hebert 2010).

These points underscore the importance of writing instruction as part of a comprehensive approach to reading and literacy instruction. Fitzgerald and Shanahan (2000) described this interrelationship when they proposed that reading and writing are independent yet reciprocal processes that share common knowledge and skills, therefore what one learns in reading can be applied to writing and vice versa. Knowledge and skills are organized into four categories: *metaknowledge*: establishing a purpose, self-monitoring, self-evaluating; *domain knowledge*: vocabulary, topical/content knowledge; *text attributes*: mechanics, grammar, text structure; and *procedural knowledge*: knowing how to approach the writing task, constructing and generating meaning, analyzing, critiquing (Jouhar and Rupley 2020).

The development of writing abilities begins early; the elementary grades lay the foundation, but explicit writing instruction with secondary students is critical for continued success in both reading and writing. Emphasizing writing in all content areas enhances learning and develops critical thinking skills. Students are more likely to retain information they read when they write about it (Graham and Hebert 2010). The more students write, the better they read; the more students read, the better they write.

The Role of Purpose, Genre, and Process

Writing is a complex, cognitive, self-directed, goal-driven activity that communicates thoughts and ideas (Graham et al. 2012a). Knowledge and practice of the purpose of writing, the genres of writing, and the writing process facilitate independence and skill in writing. This type of knowledge *about* writing helps students become more effective writers themselves. Understanding purpose is key to effective writing as writers consider what they wish to share, the medium and genre appropriate for the task, and to whom they are writing. Students must have practice in writing for a variety of purposes, learning how to argue and persuade through writing, convey information, respond to literature, share an experience, or tell stories for the purpose of entertaining an audience. Each of these purposes reflects the various genres of writing, and each genre connects reading and writing skills differently, relying on a variety of skills and strategies in both unique and complementary ways.

In grades 6–12, making connections between reading and writing when attending to genre is critical and effective. Students spend most of their time in school reading, focused on comprehension. Make use of the knowledge and skills they have acquired regarding text genre and text structure to enhance writing instruction. Students taught to recognize key words and structures when reading across the disciplines can apply this to their own writing. Students can use key words, phrases, and vocabulary from reading to enhance written response to text and the composition of longer, original writing in response to prompts. Making use of mentor texts is highly effective with secondary writers. A mentor text shows students how to write well and can allow them to envision the kind of writing they are expected to produce and want to create (Dorfman and Cappelli 2007). Including exemplars of diverse writing quality should be considered when choosing mentor texts. Helping students recognize the distinctions in quality of writing can improve their own writing skills (Graham et al. 2017).

> Knowledge and practice of the purpose of writing, the genres of writing, and the writing process facilitate independence and skill in writing. This type of knowledge *about* writing helps students become more effective writers themselves.

The writing process allows a writer to take a piece of writing from the beginning, the generation of ideas, to the end, producing a published work. Emphasis on writing as a process develops strategic writers. This process includes planning, drafting, sharing, revising/editing, publishing, and reflection/evaluation. Effective writers are strategic writers and can use these components flexibly as guidelines and guideposts for accomplishing writing tasks. Research demonstrates that providing explicit instruction in each component of the writing process, in general and related to specific genres, can help students develop as effective writers (Graham et al. 2012b; Koster et al. 2015). A Model-Practice-Reflect instructional cycle in which students observe a strategy in use (often using mentor texts), practice the strategy with their own writing, and then evaluate both their writing and their use of the strategy is supported in the research (Graham et al. 2017).

The Writing Process

Writing for meaning and expressing oneself to others is intricate and complex work. Using the writing process helps the writer take a piece of writing from the beginning, or brainstorming, to the end, or the published piece. This process is especially important to follow as students write reports, essays, and other assignments. The process at the emergent writing level is usually conducted as a group, though on occasion it is done individually. Students in higher grades who have more familiarity with the writing process can complete it individually.

There are different points to consider at each step of the writing process.

Prewriting

This is the phase during which all writing begins. At this stage, writers generate ideas, brainstorm topics, web ideas together, or talk and think about ideas. Teachers explain that students may get writing ideas from personal experiences, stories, pictures, television, websites, social media, and a variety of other sources.

This phase sets the foundation for a specific piece of writing. Students need to have a clear understanding of a writing assignment (i.e., the prompt) before they are expected to write or report on it. Before brainstorming or prewriting can begin, students need instruction on the genre or format (research report, journal entry, visual presentation, etc.), audience (the teacher, classmates, their families, the school community, etc.), and purpose (to explain, to persuade, to inform, etc.). These elements impact the types of information to brainstorm.

What does prewriting look like?

- analyzing the prompt
- researching a chosen topic, using print and digital sources
- analyzing the characteristics of the intended genre
- examining sample writing pieces
- discussing the topic with the teacher, a partner, or the class
- brainstorming ideas about the topic
- discussing the assessment tool
- creating a graphic organizer to organize ideas and the structure of the writing

Drafting

At the drafting stage of the writing process, students begin to put their ideas on paper. Students need to keep in mind the genre or format, audience, and purpose. For beginning writers, pictures and drawings are usually part of the composition. Teachers should encourage students to write as much as they can on their own throughout the writing process.

Some students struggle with writing in an orderly manner. Graphic organizers, notes, or outlines from the prewriting stage can help students sequence and organize their writing.

What does drafting look like?

- oral rehearsal of what will be written
- focusing on simply putting ideas on paper
- working fairly quickly
- leaving blank spaces for missing words
- approximating spelling
- using notes or graphic organizers to stay focused

Revising/Editing

This phase of writing consists of two parts: revising looks at the organization and structure of the writing, while editing looks at the mechanics of the writing. Students must understand how to do both. When revising, students analyze their writing for the required traits: sequencing words in a step-by-step process, descriptive language in a fictional story, topic sentences and supporting details in a persuasive piece. They also ask questions of their writing: *Does it make sense? Is anything out of order? Should anything be added or deleted?* When editing, students analyze their writing for correct spelling, grammar, and punctuation.

What do revising and editing look like?

- reading the piece aloud to confirm that it makes sense
- adding missing information
- deleting unnecessary, incorrect, or duplicate information
- proofreading for spelling, capitalization, grammar, and punctuation
- self-analysis by students
- conferences with peers or the teacher

Publishing

Publishing allows students to write for an authentic audience and celebrate their hard work. It occurs after the other steps are completed and the student is ready to produce the final copy, which can be handwritten or typed. The goal is to present the written information attractively so others can enjoy it.

What does publishing look like?

- creating a final copy
- adding illustrations, borders, a cover, and so on
- sharing orally
- posting on a classroom website, a blog, a social media site, or another platform

Ensuring that students understand the purpose for crafting a piece of writing and the elements of the genre, along with consistently providing students time to work through the process of writing, will allow them to hone their craft. As they develop as writers, they will become better at expressing their thoughts and ideas within the different genres.

The Role of Conventions, Organization, and Expression

As discussed previously, when students have a firm command of the foundations of reading, they can better attend to comprehension of a text. Similarly with writing, when foundational writing skills are in place, more time and attention can be spent on the craft of writing (Graham et al. 2012b). Vocabulary and morphology knowledge can give students freedom and flexibility over word choice and expression that can allow them to write more freely as opposed to struggling over the choice and spelling of specific words while composing. In the secondary grades, conventions instruction can concentrate on generating increasingly complex and sophisticated sentences and producing interesting, well-organized writing. In short, we can develop the traits of effective writing.

Joan Sedita (2019) identifies five strands that contribute to skilled writing:

- **Critical thinking**—Critical thinking and executive functioning, awareness of the writing process, the use of background knowledge
- **Syntax**—How sentences work
- **Text structure**—Types of texts, paragraph structures, organizational patterns, linking and transition words
- **Writing craft**—Word choice, audience, and literary devices
- **Transcription**—Spelling, handwriting, and keyboarding

Effective instruction that supports organization, expression, and proper use of conventions includes the use of mentor texts, embedded writing tasks, and instruction in writing at the sentence level (Hochman and Wexler 2017; Tompkins 2018).

Encouraging Developing Writers

A primary consideration for all instruction with students in middle and high school is fostering student interest and motivation, which are promoted by writing tasks that are authentic and meaningful. Cultivating a community of writers in an environment that supports and develops effective writers also fosters motivation. Finding opportunities to weave together purposeful writing opportunities and text is critical. Writing can be used to explain and communicate learning and understanding, as a response to reading, and as writer's craft. Many of the same practices of good readers are also done by good writers: they set goals, make predictions, make inferences, and read selectively. The more students write, the more skilled they will become in both reading and writing. Older students appreciate opportunities to work with peers during writing. They can share their work, help one another develop ideas, revise, edit, and publish their writing. Here are some characteristics of effective writers that can inform instructional considerations for developing strong writers in your classroom:

- Writers write all the time. The more experience one has writing, the better writer one becomes. Learning to write takes practice and more practice!

- Writers read a lot. Reading provides a great model for writers as to what the finished product looks like. Students who read will know how to write better than those who do not.

- Writers are aware of correct spelling. These writers use all the resources available and understand the limitations of spell-check programs.

- Writers appreciate critiques and feedback. These writers have a "thick skin" and ask for input and suggestions from many different sources.

- Writers keep a record of their learning and ideas in journals or learning logs. These records can be used to store good writing ideas, document what is being learned, activate prior knowledge, and question what is being learned (Brozo and Simpson 2003; Fisher and Frey 2004). This can also help students avoid writer's block.

- Writers compose for a variety of purposes. Learning to write in a variety of formats makes for a well-rounded, experienced writer. Writers explore different types of writing formats.

- Writers read and edit other people's writing. Such writers look for opportunities to work with others to improve their writing. Peer editing groups are an excellent way to get feedback and reinforcement from peers. This feedback is important for the self-image of the writer (Gahn 1989). Editing others' work will also help students recognize writing errors, such as an off-topic response, a weak topic sentence, a lack of supporting detail, weak vocabulary, and errors in spelling or grammar.

- Writers think objectively. They are able to step back and really look at their writing.
- Writers read their work aloud! Many errors or additions are discovered when a student listens to the writing being read aloud.

The strategies that follow are designed to support the development of writers. They support flexible, generic structures, processes, and procedures intended to become a regular part of your writing instruction and writing routines.

Genre Analysis

Objectives

- Produce clear and coherent writing in which the development, organization, and style are appropriate to task, purpose, and audience.

Background Information

Genre Analysis engages students in examining a mentor text to understand how that type of text is written. As students develop their writing skills, it is essential they deepen their understanding of the ways audience, purpose, and content set the goals for and influence the forms of writing. Genre Analysis helps students learn about the organization, goals, and functions of a particular genre, including the ways authors use stylistic elements and conventions of a genre. When using a genre approach to writing, introduce one genre at a time using Genre Analysis. As subsequent lessons or units address additional genres, make connections between genre and purpose by exploring ways a subject can cross genres to reach different audiences. Once students are familiar with the characteristics of a specific genre, they can compose their own texts in a specific genre. This strategy is adapted from activities in Beverly Derewianka's excellent resource on genre *Exploring How Texts Works* (2020).

Materials

- *Genre Analysis* (pages 136–137)
- examples of a specific writing genre

Process

1. Choose a writing genre to analyze. Select a mentor text or collect several strong examples of the genre in the form of short stories, reports, articles, student writing, and so on. Provide a copy of *Genre Analysis* for each student.

2. Explain to students that we can better understand different genres of writing by thinking about what the author is doing in a particular text. We can examine text and ask ourselves the following questions:

    - How is the text organized? (Is it a book written in chapters? A letter with a greeting and closing? Informational writing with headings and subheadings? A recount of an event? An argument? An explanation?)
    - What do you think this text might be used for?
    - Who is the audience for this text? What makes you think that?

- What do you think the writer is doing? What does the beginning tell us about the text?
- What kind of language is used? What do you notice about the sentences and words?
  - How long are the sentences?
  - What type of punctuation do you see?
  - Are there quotation marks?
  - Do you see any signal words?
  - Do you see any of the same words used many times?
  - Is it past tense? Present tense?
  - Formal or casual?

3. Place students in groups and give each group a copy of the text or one example from a collection of genre examples. Allow time for students to work collaboratively to analyze and explore the text, considering the questions on the activity sheet.

4. Bring the students back together to share the results of the analysis. Based on the discussion, create a class anchor chart that outlines the features of the genre. Ask students to tell how what they learned will inform their writing.

Differentiation

The activity can be used as a whole-class lesson, guiding students step by step through each question if students are not yet ready to analyze more independently in small groups. As students become more familiar with the genres, they can be moved toward more independence. Extend the activity for students with more advanced knowledge of genre by having them collect and share examples of a genre and eventually evaluate their own and their peers' writing based on their understanding of the genre.

Genre Analysis *Example*

Genre: Commentary and argument

Questions	My Notes
How is the text organized?	Multiple paragraphs Begins with a question for the reader and then presents a position or a thesis Each paragraph explains a reason that supports the position
What do you think we might use this text for? What makes you think that?	I think we would use this to share an opinion on a topic and to make an argument to convince others we are right. I think this because it seems to be "making a case" for their opinion.
Who is the audience for this text? What makes you think that?	The audience for this seems to be high school students who are wondering if going to college is the right choice. I think this because the author is discussing some of the common questions people have about if college is worth it.
Read the beginning of the text. What do you think the writer is doing? What does the beginning tell us about the text?	The writer is trying to connect with the audience by saying "we have all surely spent time wondering if we are choosing college because we are 'supposed to' or because it is indeed the right choice for us." I think this tells us that the writer will discuss some of the reasons teenagers might feel this way, that she is going to make a choice and tells us her reasons.
What kind of language is used? What do you notice about the sentences and words? How long are the sentences? What type of punctuation do you see? Are there quotation marks? Do you see any signal words? Do you see any of the same words used many times? Is it past tense? Present tense? Formal or casual?	The sentences are pretty short and direct, I think she is trying to be clear. There are many question marks since she is writing about the questions, and she puts a lot of things in quotation marks—like the sarcastic kind. It seems pretty casual because she is trying to connect with a teenage audience.

Name: _____ Date: _____

Genre Analysis

Directions: Examine the mentor text. Respond to the questions to learn more about the genre.

Genre: _____

Questions	My Notes
How is the text organized?	
What do you think we might use this text for? What makes you think that?	
Who is the audience for this text? What makes you think that?	
Read the beginning of the text. What do you think the writer is doing? What does the beginning tell us about the text?	

Name: _____ Date:_____

Genre Analysis (continued)

Directions: Examine the mentor text. Respond to the questions to learn more about the genre.

Genre: _____

Questions	My Notes
What kind of language is used? What do you notice about the sentences and words? How long are the sentences?	
What type of punctuation do you see? Are there quotation marks?	
Do you see any signal words? Do you see any of the same words used many times?	
Is it past tense? Present tense? Formal or casual?	

© Shell Education   Literacy Strategies—131699

WRITING: GENRE CHARACTERISTICS

EASE (Examine, Assess, Suggest, Envision)

Objectives

- Interpret words and phrases as they are used in a text, including determining technical, connotative, and figurative meanings, and analyze how specific word choices shape meaning or tone.
- Analyze the structure of texts, including how specific sentences, paragraphs, and larger portions of the text relate to each other and the whole.
- Draw evidence from literary or informational texts to support analysis, reflection, and research.

Background Information

EASE (Dollins 2020) is a strategy to develop writing skills through critical analysis of mentor texts. The strategy scaffolds this analysis by asking a series of guiding questions students can use to adopt or adapt specific author moves in their own writing (Dollins 2020). Mentor texts are valuable because they serve as examples of good writing that students can learn from, be inspired by, and emulate. They can be published works from professional writers or examples of teacher and peer writing. Teachers can share mentor texts that provide examples of nearly any trait of good writing, any genre, and any text structure. Rhetorical styles, literary devices, word choice, syntax, and grammar usage can all be studied through analysis of mentor texts. Developing writers should be immersed in mentor texts and return to them again and again to "learn how to do what they may not yet be able to do on their own" (Dorfman and Cappelli 2007, 2).

Materials

- *EASE (Examine, Assess, Suggest, Envision)* (page 141)
- text selection

Process

1. Select a mentor text that exemplifies a writing feature or technique that is the focus for your writing instruction. Choose a text students can read that models easily identifiable techniques or approaches to writing and shows students how to write well (Dorfman and Cappelli 2007). Be explicit about what you want students to identify in the text. The focus might be features of the genre, author's craft "moves," word choice, or grammar. Explicitly teach that language feature or function.

2. Read, or have students read, the mentor text or an excerpt. (If possible, provide students with individual copies of the text; however, students in groups may share copies, or you may read aloud to the class.)

3. Distribute the *EASE* activity sheets and explain the strategy. Students will analyze the text and consider the following questions.

   - **Examine:** What does the author do? What writing move do they make? For example, does the author use figurative language? First-person point of view? Repetition?
   - **Assess:** Why did the author write this way? How does the craft affect the audience? Does the craft affect the meaning? The tone? The voice?
   - **Suggest:** How could you write that part in a different way? How can you keep the meaning but present it differently?
   - **Envision:** When could you use a similar move in your writing? In what genres could you use it? What would it look like?

4. Model the EASE strategy with a portion of the text. Think aloud as you identify the craft move and think through the steps of EASE.

5. Have students work in pairs or independently to identify another move in the text and think through the steps of EASE.

6. Invite pairs or individual students to share with the class.

7. When students are familiar with EASE, have them use the *EASE* activity sheets for guidance as they apply the analyzed moves to their own writing.

Differentiation

Students may benefit from working in pairs and small groups until they are familiar with EASE. Scaffold this strategy by working with students to identify the craft moves or providing students with an example of the move at the beginning of the lesson. Students who demonstrate advanced skills in writing or identifying craft moves can begin applying EASE to their own writing after the initial lesson.

EASE (Examine, Assess, Suggest, Envision) Example

Text: The Raven

Author: Edgar Allan Poe

Page: _____

Passage or Excerpt: Once upon a midnight dreary while I pondered weak and weary (line 1)
Doubting, dreaming dreams no mortal ever dared to dream before (line 19-20)

Examine What does the author do?	Poe uses alliteration throughout the poem—he uses words that start with the same sound.
Assess Why did the author write this way?	It draws the reader's attention to certain words. "The Raven" is a poem, and so the sound like the rhyme and rhythm is important. The words he uses also set the mood and the tone for the reader.
Suggest How could you write the passage in a different way?	Once late at night I was tired and bored with life. It definitely changes the meaning and the effect, so I wouldn't change it like this for a poem.
Envision When could you use a similar move in your own writing?	I could use this in my own writing when I want to make a dramatic effect or really capture the reader's attention if I was writing a poem. My example: I sighed sadly at the thought of my silent solitude.

(Adapted from Dollins 2020)

Name: _____ Date: _____

EASE (Examine, Assess, Suggest, Envision)

Directions: Read the text and find examples of author's craft. Answer the EASE questions to closely examine the author's craft.

Text: _____

Author: _____

Page: _____

Passage or Excerpt: _____

_____

_____

_____

Examine What does the author do?	
Assess Why did the author write this way?	
Suggest How could you write the passage in a different way?	
Envision When could you use a similar move in your own writing?	

Source: Adapted from Dollins 2020

WRITING: GENRE CHARACTERISTICS

RAFT

Objectives

- Produce clear and coherent writing in which the development and organization are appropriate to task, purpose, and audience.

Background Information

RAFT stands for Role, Audience, Format, and Topic—key ingredients of writing assignments (Santa, Havens, and Valdes 1995). RAFT is a strategy to help students understand their roles as writers, the audiences they will write for, and how to communicate their ideas effectively across varied formats and purposes for writing. Developing a sense of purpose and audience is key in effective communication. RAFT writing supports students in considering topics from multiple perspectives, thinking and writing creatively, and developing understanding of main ideas, coherence, and elaboration in writing. RAFT prompts can be designed in ways that require students to write from a perspective other than their own, strengthening their critical and creative thinking skills. RAFT can be implemented in any content area and used for traditional forms of writing as well as formats such as posters, brochures, and multimedia.

Materials

- *RAFT* (page 144)
- sample writing selection

Process

1. Select a short piece of writing with clear, easily identifiable RAFT components. Tell your students that writers need to consider specific elements before they write. Lead a discussion to identify the following elements in the piece:
   - **Role:** Who or what is the writer?
   - **Audience:** To whom is the author writing?
   - **Format:** What is the format of the writing?
   - **Topic and strong verb:** What is the writing about? What is the purpose of this communication? (the strong verb indicates purpose and tone)

2. Display the *RAFT* activity sheet and brainstorm with the class a sample RAFT prompt, recording suggestions and determining a role, audience, format, topic, and strong verb. It may be necessary to model how to write responses to a RAFT prompt.

3. Have students work in small groups or individually to write in response to the RAFT prompt.

4. As students become familiar with RAFT, have them develop a RAFT prompt on their own and then write to the prompt. Alternatively, you can provide part or all of a RAFT prompt for practice, scaffolding students' choices until they are ready to work independently.

Differentiation

Introduce each component of RAFT separately to allow students to develop command over each one before moving to the next. Provide multiple choices for one of the components to demonstrate how varying the elements can change the writing. For example, the prompt could have one Role, one Audience, and one Topic, but several Formats. Challenge advanced students to develop their own RAFT prompts and begin writing independently.

Name: _____ Date: _____

RAFT

Directions: Use this planner to organize your RAFT Assignment.

Role:	Audience:

Format:	Topic:

My Writing

Expository Writing Frames

Objectives

- Analyze the structure an author uses to organize a text, including how the major sections contribute to the whole and to the development of the ideas.
- Write informative/explanatory texts to examine a topic and convey ideas, concepts, and information through the selection, organization, and analysis of relevant content.
- Draw evidence from literary or informational texts to support analysis, reflection, and research.

Background Information

Students in grades 6 to 12 are expected to produce writing across the content areas, often in response to reading complex text. Expository Writing Frames are effective scaffolds for such writing. Though we may think of frames as scaffolds for students in elementary grades, their use is strongly recommended for adolescent readers and writers and even postsecondary students (Graff and Birkenstein 2014). Writing frames build students' confidence and support them as they learn the structure and organization of the five key text types. Using a skeleton of a few sentences, words, or phrases common to a genre allows writers to focus attention on their thoughts. Writers can use frames to write single paragraphs or put them together for essays, reports, stories, and other writing. As students advance in their writing skills, paragraph frames can be used to further develop word choice and elaboration skills.

Materials

- writing frame (page 147 or teacher-created)
- text selection

Process

1. Develop a prompt for the task you wish students to engage in. Select or create a corresponding writing frame. Sample frames are provided on page 147, but you may wish to create your own frame based on a specific text. Note that this strategy works well in conjunction with Text Structure Analysis (page 70). In that case, students can refer to the graphic organizer they used during Text Structure Analysis to organize a written response to the reading.

2. Review with students a piece of text with a structure that mirrors the frame. This can be a new text, or you can revisit a text used for Text Structure Analysis.

3. Display the prompt and the writing frame. Share the prompt, and introduce the frame and discuss its elements. Help students make connections between the language and structure of the frame and the text structure.

4. Have students use the frame to respond to the prompt. This can be done as a whole class, or students can work with partners and then share ideas with the class. Encourage students to elaborate, include long and short sentences, and use target vocabulary if appropriate.

Differentiation

Writing frames can be differentiated for students by complexity. Some students may benefit from initial practice using shorter frames. Students with stronger analysis skills can use more complex frames or may not need frames to respond to the prompt.

Expository Writing Frames

Description

1. A _____ is a type of _____. It is made up of _____ and looks like _____. Some _____ have _____ such as _____. For example, _____.

2. _____ has several characteristics. One characteristic is _____. Another is _____, which is important because _____.

Sequence

1. First, _____. Then _____. Next _____. Finally, _____.

2. To begin with, _____. After that, _____. Lastly, _____.

3. _____ happened. Prior to that _____. Then _____. After that, _____. In the end, _____.

Compare and Contrast

1. There are many similarities/differences between _____ and _____. For example, they both _____. *OR* For example, _____ but _____.

2. _____ and _____ are alike in several ways. Both _____. On the other hand, one way they differ is _____. While they share _____, another difference is _____.

Cause and Effect

1. The effects of _____ are important because _____. One effect of _____ is _____. Another is _____. Because of these results, it important that _____.

2. Since _____ was _____. This is significant because _____.

3. The causes of _____ were _____. If _____ hadn't happened _____, then, _____. Because this occurred, _____. It helps to explain why, _____ which is important because _____.

Problem/Solution

1. _____ is a problem because _____. One possible solution is _____. This solution should be considered because _____. Therefore, _____. As a result, _____.

2. A solution to effectively address the problem of _____ is _____. This is an effective solution because _____. A potential pitfall is _____. However, _____.

WRITING: GENRE CHARACTERISTICS

Scholarly Texts

Objective

- Write informative/explanatory texts to examine and convey complex ideas and information clearly and accurately.

Background Information

Scholarly Texts is a strategy to help students develop academic voice in their writing. In grades 6–12, students engage in many writing tasks that require synthesizing multiple sources; providing reliable evidence; and establishing credibility for their theses, opinions, and arguments. These tasks require what is referred to as an "academic voice." Scholarly Texts supports students in making the transition from everyday, less formal language to writing using the hallmarks of academic writing: unbiased, formal, declarative, precise, and supported by evidence. This strategy lends itself to a variety of explicit lessons on voice, sentence structure, word choice, and the use of academic language. It draws on students' experience condensing their thoughts and communicating in an informal, casual style through texting.

Materials

- *Scholarly Texts* (page 151)

Process

1. Provide students with a model of a statement made using a casual, informal voice and the same statement conveyed in an academic voice. Have students compare and contrast the two statements.

2. Explain to students that when we write for scholarly purposes, we want to use an academic voice. Discuss the elements of academic voice:

   - Uses declarative statements
   - Avoids casual language
   - Is concise
   - Uses precise words and specific vocabulary
   - Uses evidence

3. Distribute copies of the *Scholarly Texts* activity sheet and explain how to use it: Write a brief, texting-style message, as if to a friend, that shares a belief or feelings about a topic. Alternately, you could describe a vocabulary term or concept using everyday language. The goal is to convey a message using informal language—as when texting.

4. Think aloud as you rewrite the text as a "scholarly text," attending to the hallmarks of academic voice in your writing. Focus on the content of the message and alternative ways to convey the same ideas.

5. Assign students to work with partners and give them instructions for writing a new text message, as if to a friend. Have partners work together to reply to that text with a "scholarly text."

6. Allow time for pairs to share their texts with another pair or with the class.

7. Provide additional practice by repeating the process.

Differentiation

This strategy can be scaffolded by providing examples of the informal texts and having students translate them into scholarly texts. Students who need minimal support with this strategy can work independently to generate their own messages to "translate" to academic language. Or, they can work with partners and exchange messages to translate.

Scholarly Texts Example

Academic Voice

- ❏ Make declarative statements.
- ❏ Avoid casual language.
- ❏ Be concise.
- ❏ Use precise words and specific vocabulary.
- ❏ Use evidence.

I think school uniforms are good for students because then we don't worry about who is wearing what designer brand.

School uniforms are beneficial because they eliminate the focus on designer labels.

There have been a lot of studies that showed students fight less when they go to a school with school uniforms.

Research demonstrates school uniforms reduce behavior problems.

Most students don't like to wear uniforms because they can't show their off their sense of style at school.

A majority of students believe uniforms restrict self-expression.

Name: _____ Date: _____

Scholarly Texts

Directions: Write about the topic in an everyday voice as if you were texting your idea to a friend. Then write about it using a more formal, academic voice.

Academic Voice

- ❑ Make declarative statements.
- ❑ Avoid casual language.
- ❑ Be concise.
- ❑ Use precise words and specific vocabulary.
- ❑ Use evidence.

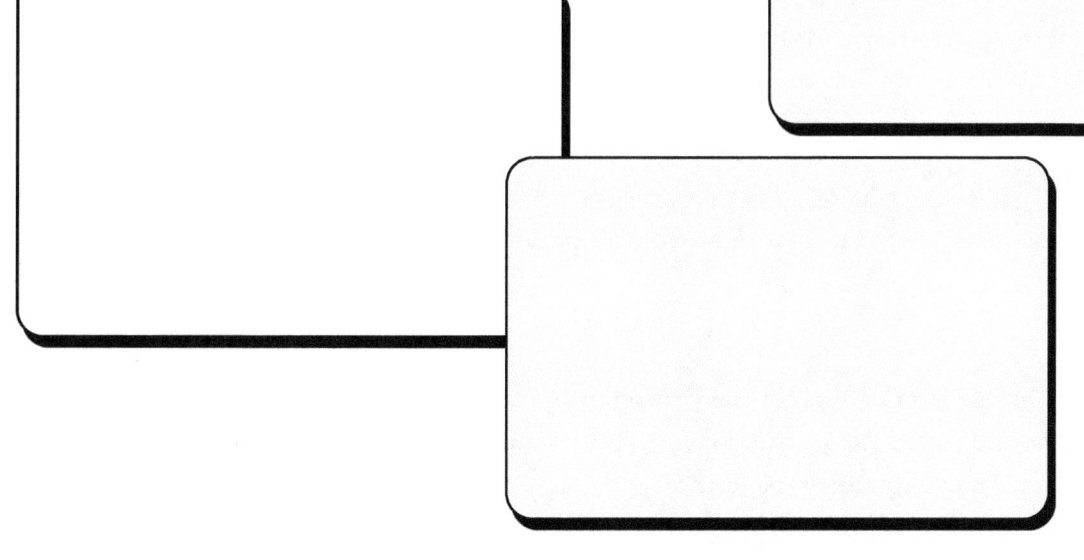

© Shell Education   Literacy Strategies—131699   **151**

WRITING: PREWRITING AND ORGANIZATION

Planning for Writing

Objectives

- Produce clear and coherent writing in which the development, organization, and style are appropriate to task, purpose, and audience.
- With some guidance and support from peers and adults, develop and strengthen writing as needed by planning, revising, editing, rewriting, or trying a new approach.

Background Information

Planning is an essential step in the writing process. Writers in middle and high school should be taught an organized and purposeful approach to brainstorming, sorting and selecting ideas, considering purpose and audience, and gathering information prior to writing. Prewriting activities harness both the power of rehearsal to spark creativity and the effectiveness of more formal prewriting to help students organize their thoughts and plan for writing. These can be highly effective for reluctant writers or students who struggle to get their "creative juices flowing" or find their voice when faced with a writing task. The focus on narrowing and organizing helps students develop into more strategic writers (Tompkins 2018). Several organizers and mnemonic devices to support students during the planning stage are included here (Graham et al. 2017).

Materials

- planning organizer to match assignment (see pages 154–156)

Process

1. Prepare by selecting a focus for the writing unit. If using the genre approach, select the genre and gather the instructional support materials needed. Open the unit with the Genre Analysis strategy (page 133).

2. Select a planning mnemonic or organizer that supports the genre. The organizers correspond with the following genres:
   - PLAN Organizer: Informational and Persuasive (page 154)
   - STOP Organizer: Persuasive (page 155)
   - Story Arc: Narrative (page 156)

3. Explain to students that effective writers take time to plan their writing and organize their thoughts before they begin to compose in the drafting stage. Show and explain the mnemonic or the elements of the organizer. Direct students to review the selected organizer and think about how they can prepare for writing by planning.

4. Direct students to plan their writing using the mnemonic or organizer.

5. Have students share their planning with partners. Once they have completed this step, they may move to the drafting phase of the writing process.

Differentiation

Students may initially need extensive modeling and scaffolding of this stage of the writing process. Providing students with mentor texts and engaging in backwards mapping may help. Deconstructing mentor texts can illuminate the planning and organization behind the writing. Students may need support in transferring ideas to the graphic organizers. Encourage advanced students to self-select an appropriate organizer, and when complete, move to the drafting phase.

Name: _____ Date: _____

PLAN Organizer

Directions: Use this planner to organize your assignment.

Pay attention to the writing assignment: What are you asked to write about?		
List your main ideas after doing some thinking/ information gathering.	**A**dd supporting ideas/details to each main idea.	**N**umber the order of your ideas.

Source: De La Paz and Graham 2002

154 Literacy Strategies—131699 © Shell Education

Name: _____ Date: _____

STOP Organizer

Directions: Use this planner to organize your assignment.

Suspend judgment and consider each side of the issue. List ideas for each side.

Side A	Side B

Take a side: Circle the side you will make an argument for.

Organize your ideas. Decide which ideas are strong and put a star next to the ideas you will use. Put an X next to ideas you will refute.

Plan more as you write. Use the space below to jot down additional ideas.

Source: Kiuhara et al. 2012

Name: _____ Date: _____

Story Arc

Directions: Use this planner to organize your assignment.

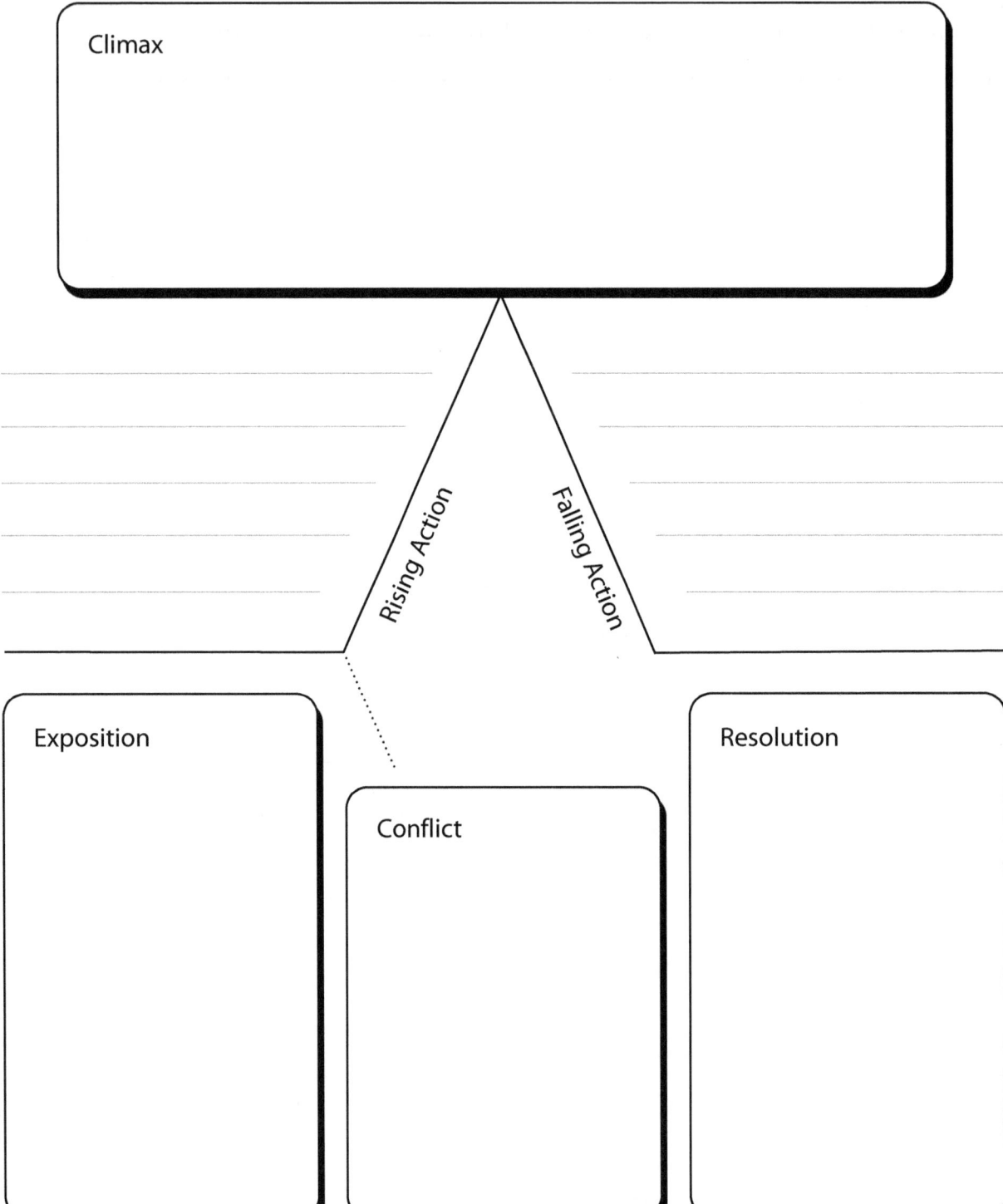

Composing a Draft

Objectives

- Produce clear and coherent writing in which the development, organization, and style are appropriate to task, purpose, and audience.
- With some guidance and support from peers and adults, develop and strengthen writing as needed by planning, revising, editing, rewriting, or trying a new approach.

Background Information

Drafting, the second stage of the writing process, is when students expand their planning ideas and notes into a rough working draft. Students further explore their ideas and the writing task as they build upon their initial plans. Drafting is an iterative process, requiring students to continually return to their draft to elaborate, clarify, and redraft. As with other stages in the writing process, drafting creates opportunities for teaching and learning cycles. Teachers can provide explicit instruction and model how to turn ideas from planning into complete, interesting sentences and how to form introductions, body paragraphs, and conclusions. Writers in middle and high school should be taught strategies for creating strong leads, attending to audience and genre, and writing sentences for different purposes. Several mnemonic devices to support students during the drafting stage are included here (Graham et al. 2017).

Materials

- drafting guide to match assignment (see pages 159–161)

Process

1. Prepare for the lesson by identifying a focus for explicit instruction related to composing drafts. These include reviewing a mentor text, teaching strategies for translating ideas into strong sentences such as color-coding words and phrases in planning notes that can be combined into sentences, and instruction on how to draft topic sentences, sentences that express supporting details, concluding statements, and so on.
2. Remind students of the goal of the writing task and give them time to review their planning notes.
3. Explain to students that effective writers use the drafting stage to turn their planning ideas into a working piece of writing. Introduce and discuss the elements of the guide you selected. Direct students to review the guide and think about how they can

prepare for writing the working draft. If necessary, review a mentor text and analyze for the components of the mnemonic in the guide.

4. Provide explicit instruction on the focus lesson related to drafting.

5. Give students time to work on their drafts, using the guide. The drafting stage may require multiple class sessions.

6. Have students share their initial drafts with partners.

Differentiation

Students may initially need extensive modeling and scaffolding of this stage of the writing process. Deconstructing mentor texts can illuminate the planning and organization behind the writing. Some students will benefit from the use of paragraph or sentence frames. Students with strong writing skills may use the organizers to evaluate and analyze their writing once they have composed an initial draft (rather than using it with mentor text).

Name: _____ Date: _____

DARE

Directions: Use this process to write a draft.

> **Genres: Persuasive, Argumentative**
>
> ☐ **D**evelop a topic statement to support your thesis.
> ☐ **A**dd supporting ideas to support your thesis.
> ☐ **R**eject possible arguments on the other side.
> ☐ **E**nd with a conclusion.

_____
_____
_____
_____
_____
_____
_____
_____
_____
_____
_____
_____
_____
_____
_____

Source: Kiuhara et al. 2012

Name: _____ Date: _____

WRITE

Directions: Use this process to write a draft.

> **Genre: Any**
>
> ❑ **W**ork from your plan.
> ❑ **R**emember your goals.
> ❑ **I**nclude transition words for each paragraph.
> ❑ **T**ry to use different kinds of sentences.
> ❑ **E**xciting, interesting words

_____
_____
_____
_____
_____
_____
_____
_____
_____
_____
_____

Source: De La Paz and Graham 2002

Name: _____ Date: _____

C-SPACE

Directions: Use these elements to write a draft.

Genre: Narrative

- ❑ **C**haracters
- ❑ **S**etting
- ❑ **P**urpose of what the main character tries to do
- ❑ **A**ction to achieve goal
- ❑ **C**onclusion of action
- ❑ **E**motions of main character

_____
_____
_____
_____
_____
_____
_____
_____
_____
_____
_____
_____
_____
_____

Source: Harris et al. 2008

WRITING: PREWRITING AND ORGANIZATION

R.A.C.E. Organizer

Objectives
- Draw evidence from literary or informational texts to support analysis, reflection, and research.

Background Information
The R.A.C.E. Organizer is a tool for composing written responses to text. In grades 6–12, students are expected to develop the skills to produce high quality responses to literature and informational text. While it is common to teach students to write essays and narrative pieces, explicit instruction in constructed response to text is often overlooked. Students need explicit instruction to write organized, meaningful responses that connect and integrate information from several sources, refer to textual evidence, and cite supporting examples. These responses assess both reading comprehension and writing. This organizer reminds students of the components of quality responses to text by giving them a process to follow while constructing responses. The organizer can be used across all content areas and lends itself to use with a wide variety of texts.

Materials
- *R.A.C.E. Organizer* (page 165)
- text selection

Process
1. Choose an appropriate text to model the process of writing a response using the organizer. You may wish to begin with a simpler, shorter text to scaffold practice. Develop a question and write a model response to the question to share with students. Develop a second question that students will respond to.

2. Introduce the organizer by telling students that today they will learn a mnemonic to help construct responses to text. Display the mnemonic and explain each element.

    R—Restate the question. Write it as a statement.

    A—Answer the question.

    C—Cite text evidence.

    E—Explain the text evidence/your answer.

3. Distribute the *R.A.C.E. Organizer*. Display the short piece of text you have selected and allow students time to read the text.

4. Display the question and the model response you constructed. Read them and direct students to use the R.A.C.E. mnemonic as a guide to evaluate the model response.

5. Have students discuss their thoughts with partners.

6. Display the question developed for student practice and direct students to go back to the text and answer the question using the *R.A.C.E. Organizer*.

7. Allow students time to share their notes with partners. Once they have compared notes, students may write their completed responses at the bottom of their activity sheets.

Differentiation

Students may benefit from individual lessons on each component of the R.A.C.E. mnemonic and then practice using the components together to create quality responses. Scaffold the process by providing sentence starters or sentences frames for possible responses. Several such frames can be found in the Expository Writing Frames strategy (page 145). Advanced readers and writers can move directly to writing the paragraph response rather than move through each step of the R.A.C.E. strategy.

R.A.C.E. Organizer Example

Question: How did disagreements over the power of the federal government lead to the creation of the two-party system?

Restate the question.	The two-party system in the United States was created because of disagreements over how much power the federal government should have.
Answer the question.	Alexander Hamilton believed in a strong central government, while Thomas Jefferson believed in strong states' rights. This disagreement led to the two-party system.
Cite evidence from the text.	Hamilton was a Federalist (p. 6), and Jefferson was a Democratic-Republican (p. 6). "Many historians say no event shaped the founding years of the United States as much as the personal and political rivalry between Jefferson and Hamilton" (p. 9).
Explain the text evidence.	Federalists believed in a strong central government, but the Democratic-Republicans believed in strong state governments and less central power.

The two-party system in the United States was created due to serious disagreements between the founders. On page 6, the author describes the difference between the ideas of the Federalists and the Democratic-Republicans. Alexander Hamilton was a Federalist who believed in a strong central government, while Thomas Jefferson was a Democratic-Republican who believed in strong states' rights. They had many arguments over this when they served in Washington's Cabinet. On page 9, the author tells us that many historians agree that this rivalry was very important in shaping the two-party system.

Name: _____ Date: _____

R.A.C.E. Organizer

Directions: Construct your response to the question. Use the checklist to evaluate your response.

Question: _____
_____

Restate the question.	
Answer the question.	
Cite evidence from the text.	
Explain the text evidence.	

_____
_____
_____
_____
_____

- ☐ **R**
- ☐ **A**
- ☐ **C**
- ☐ **E**

Revising Writing

Objectives

- Produce clear and coherent writing in which the development, organization, and style are appropriate to task, purpose, and audience.
- With some guidance and support from peers and adults, develop and strengthen writing as needed by planning, revising, editing, rewriting, or trying a new approach.

Background Information

Revision is a distinct and important step in the writing process. Sometimes, student writers combine revision and editing, focusing on proofreading, fixing grammar, maybe adding a few words or combining sentences. But revision should include writers looking at their drafts and asking questions about purpose, organization, and content. At its most meaningful, revision leads to significant changes to the draft. Engaging students in the revision process requires explicit teaching of revision skills and strategies. Instruction on reviewing ideas and organization and elaborating strengthens students' skills and helps demystify the process. Working with peers is effective, as students can apply reflection questions and revision skills to the work of a classmate, not just to their own writing. Two mnemonic devices to support students during the revision stage are included here (Graham et al. 2017).

Materials

- revision guide to match assignment (see pages 168–170)

Process

1. Prepare for the lesson by selecting a focus for explicit instruction during the revision process. One approach is to focus on the criteria specific to the genre students are working in. Another approach is to select one aspect of the STAR guide (page 168) for an explicit revision mini-lesson.
2. Explain to students that effective writers spend significant time reflecting on and revising their working drafts. In fact, many professional writers follow a motto of "A good writer is a rewriter." Show and explain the mnemonic guide. Direct students to review the guide and think about how they might approach revision.
3. Provide explicit instruction on the focus for revision.
4. Allow students time to work on revising their writing using the guide. You may wish to put students in pairs and have them engage in peer editing using the guide.

5. If students are reviewing one another's work, have them review the suggestions made by peers, or have students share their revisions with partners and ask for feedback. Once they have completed this step, they will move to the editing phase of the writing process.

Differentiation

Students may initially need extensive modeling and scaffolding of this stage of the writing process. Providing students with mentor texts can be a useful support. Working on revision in teacher-led small groups may also be useful when students are still learning to write independently. Challenge students with advanced writing skills to evaluate their own writing to identify a revision focus that will make their writing even stronger. Alternately, pair strong writers for peer review and have them work together to identify areas for improvement.

Name: _____ Date: _____

STAR

Directions: Review and revise your draft.

Substitute	**T**ake out	**A**dd	**R**earrange
Overused words with precise words Weak verbs with strong verbs Weak adjectives with strong adjectives Common nouns with proper nouns	Unnecessary repetitions Irrelevant information Information that belongs elsewhere	Details, descriptions, new information, figurative language, clarification of meaning Expand your ideas	Move the information for a more logical and organized flow
My notes/Peer notes	My notes/Peer notes	My notes/Peer notes	My notes/Peer notes

Source: Gallagher 2006

Name: _____ Date:_____

CDO for Sentences

Directions: Review and revise your draft.

Compare	**D**iagnose	**O**perate
Read the sentence. **Consider by asking:** Does this sentence work?	Ask the questions. Does it sound right? Is it communicating the intended meaning? Is it useful? Will the reader understand it? Will the reader be interested in what it says? Will the reader believe what it says?	**Decide how you will change the sentence.**
My notes/Peer notes	My notes/Peer notes	My notes/Peer notes

Source: De La Paz, Swanson, and Graham 1998

Name: _____ Date:_____

CDO for Paragraphs

Directions: Review and revise your draft.

Compare	**D**iagnose	**O**perate
Read the paragraph. As you read each paragraph, stop and think about what works and what doesn't work in the writing.	**Ask the questions.** Are there too few facts? Are there inaccuracies? Does the evidence support the claim? Do you explain to the reader how the evidence supports the claim? Does this paragraph belong with the rest of the paper? Is this part in the wrong order?	**How can it be fixed?** Rewrite. Add more. Leave this part out. Change the wording.
My notes/Peer notes	My notes/Peer notes	My notes/Peer notes

Source: De La Paz, Swanson, and Graham 1998

Editing Writing

Objectives

- Produce clear and coherent writing in which the development, organization, and style are appropriate to task, purpose, and audience.
- With some guidance and support from peers and adults, develop and strengthen writing as needed by planning, revising, editing, rewriting, or trying a new approach.

Background Information

Once students have gone through the revision stage of the writing process, they are ready for editing. During the editing stage, students proofread their writing. They correct mistakes of spelling, grammar, sentence structure and form, word choice, and punctuation. Teachers often act as default editors when giving feedback, but editing skills are best developed by allowing students to be their own editors. When teachers edit, students often fix mistakes with little thought to how or why they were made. Self-editing offers students the opportunity to find and correct mistakes and identify patterns in their errors, which helps prevent future mistakes. Providing tools and resources such as checklists or mnemonics helps build students' self-efficacy and ownership of editing skills. Peer editing is also useful for honing editing skills. Mnemonic devices to support students during the editing stage are included here (Graham et al. 2017).

Materials

- editing guide to match assignment (see pages 173–174)

Process

1. Prepare for the lesson by selecting a focus for explicit instruction during the editing process. One approach is to focus on the criteria found in the editing guides (pages 173–174).
2. Explain to students that effective writers engage in an editing, or proofreading, phase of the writing process after they finish revising. This is the time to look for and correct errors in spelling, grammar, and punctuation rather than reflect on the content of the writing. Direct students to review the selected editing guide and think about how they might approach editing.
3. Provide explicit instruction on the focus for editing.
4. Allow students time to work on editing their own writing or a peer's writing by using the guide.

5. If students are reviewing one another's work, have them review the edits recommended by peers, or have students share their own edits with partners. Once they have completed this step, they may be ready to publish their writing.

Differentiation

Students may initially need extensive modeling and instruction to be able to identify mistakes in grammar and improve word choice. Providing students with mini-lessons and working in small, teacher-led groups may be useful. Challenge students with advanced writing skills to evaluate their own writing to identify an editing focus that will make their writing even stronger. Alternately, pair strong writers for peer review and have them work together to identify areas for improvement.

Name: _____ Date: _____

COPS

Directions: Edit your work.

☐ **C**apitalization	Have I capitalized the first word of each sentence? Have I capitalized proper nouns—words that name specific people, places, or things?
☐ **O**rder/Organization	Are the words in the correct order? When I read a sentence aloud, does it sound right? Have I left out any words? Have I indented paragraphs? How is the overall appearance?
☐ **P**unctuation	Have I used ending punctuation correctly? Have I used punctuation marks (commas, quotation marks, colons, etc.) correctly?
☐ **S**pelling	Have I spelled all words correctly? Have I checked a spelling resource if I am unsure?

Source: Harris et al. 2008

Name: _____ Date: _____

CUPS

Directions: Edit your work.

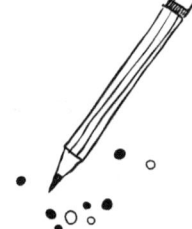

Genre: Informational, Research, Argument

☐ **C**itation	Did I give credit where credit is due? Have I paraphrased information and evidence properly? Have I provided citations for my research/evidence? • in the text? • in the references? • with page numbers?
☐ **U**sage	Are the words in the correct order? Do my subjects and verbs agree? When I read a sentence aloud, does it sound right? Have I indented paragraphs? How is the overall appearance?
☐ **P**unctuation	Have I used ending punctuation correctly? Have I used punctuation marks (commas, quotation marks, colons, etc.) correctly?
☐ **S**pelling	Have I spelled all words correctly? Have I checked a spelling resource if I am unsure?

Reading Response

Objectives
- Draw evidence from literary or informational texts to support analysis, in a reflection, and for research.

Background Information
Reading Response activities are well-established and effective techniques for helping students learn from, make connections to, and respond to text. Reading Response charts and journals can keep students engaged in reading, allow them to use writing to clarify and organize their reactions to text, and develop critical thinking and analysis skills (Au et al. 1995; Cohen 2007). Students are asked to bring a critical lens to what the text says and what the author brings to the text, and are asked to think about what they bring to the reading and what meaning they are making from the text. This is an excellent practice in literary criticism, as it allows students to interrogate their responses to texts. Reading Response helps students become more aware of their biases and when it is appropriate to use them as they critically consider other's points of view. Students can refer to these charts and journals when writing essays and other responses to text, and use them during class discussions about text. Reading Response can be used across content areas and with a wide variety of texts.

Materials
- *Reading Response* (page 178)
- text selection

Process
1. Select a text that is appropriate for this type of critical analysis. Many literary, historical, and argument-based texts work well. If Reading Response is being introduced for the first time, use a text students have already read.
2. Explain to students that they will examine the text for evidence of the author's point of view and will consider how they think and feel about this point of view.
3. Review questions students can consider that will help them interrogate their perspectives on the author's point of view. Examples include:
   - What did you already know about this topic or subject?
   - How do you feel about this topic or subject?
   - Do you like or dislike this text/point of view? Why?
   - What is the author thinking? How can you tell?

- Do you think the author has any bias or preconceptions about this topic? What are they?
- Can you connect this text to another text?

4. Draw a Reading Response chart on the board (see page 178) and model the process. Select a phrase from the text that represents the author's point of view. Write it on the left-side column of the chart. Think aloud as you construct a short response in the right-side column. Model how to reflect on your own biases, prior knowledge, and feelings about the author's point of view.

5. Distribute the *Reading Response* activity sheets. Allow students time to reread the text and write their responses to the text. Encourage students to cite text evidence when giving examples of the author's point of view.

6. Have students share their responses with partners.

Differentiation

Scaffold this activity by identifying examples of point of view for students. Some students will benefit from working on Reading Response in teacher-led small groups. Scaffolding might also be provided in the form of simple sentence starters students can use to respond. For example, *I think _____; I feel _____; While the author _____, I _____*. Students with advanced skills can generate a list of questions to ask as they read rather than depending on the questions provided by the teacher.

Reading Response Chart Example

Social Studies Example

Author's Point of View	My Thoughts
Under the rule of the Nazi Party, Jewish people faced heavy persecution. The Nazi Party took control of their businesses, confiscated their assets, dictated where they could live, and punished any dissenters. As the power of the Nazi Party grew, <u>the rest of Europe turned a blind eye to the situation</u> and failed to intercede on behalf of the Jewish people. (p. 126)	While it is true that many people ignored the anti-Semitic beliefs and actions of the Nazi Party, there were also many brave people who spoke out against the injustices they saw happening around them. Many innocent people lost their lives trying to hide Jewish people or help them escape during this time period. I do not think it is completely fair to say that all of Europe failed to acknowledge the atrocities happening under the Nazi regime.

Fiction Example for *The Great Gatsby* (Fitzgerald 1965)

Author's Point of View	My Thoughts
"His lack of formal schooling made him ignorant to the rules of civilized society." (p. 14) The author seems to say formal schooling and social intelligence are the same.	While students do learn about social interactions in school, it is not the only place where people learn how to use good manners. It is very possible to have good manners without attending formal schooling. Furthermore, there are many people that have gone through years of formal schooling and yet know very little about manners or the rules for being around others.

Name: _____ Date: _____

Reading Response Chart

Directions: As you read, write examples and evidence of the author's point of view. Record your thoughts and beliefs about the topic.

Author's Point of View	My Thoughts

WRITING: RESPONDING TO READING

Read, Reread, List, Compose (RRLC)

Objectives

- Gather relevant information from multiple print and digital sources; assess the credibility of each source; and quote or paraphrase the data and conclusions of others while avoiding plagiarism and providing basic bibliographic information for sources.

Background Information

Read, Reread, List, Compose (RRLC) is a strategy to support development of academic writing skills (Kettel and DeFauw 2018). Writing informational essays, arguments, and research reports in middle school and beyond requires that students be able to gather information from a variety of sources and summarize and paraphrase while avoiding plagiarism. In both paraphrasing and summarizing, the writer puts the author's ideas into their own words, but paraphrasing emphasizes one portion of text, while summarization attends to the entirety of the text (Kettel and De Fauw 2018). Both skills can and should be taught explicitly in grades 6–12. RRLC supports students in writing about their reading and avoiding plagiarism.

Materials

- *Read, Reread, List, Compose* (page 182)
- text selections

Process

1. Plan to complete this lesson over several class sessions. Prepare for the lesson by selecting two or three texts on a particular topic. They should be relatively short texts students can read and reread to take notes. If students have access to the internet, select at least one web-based text.

2. Explain to students that Read, Reread, List, Compose (RRLC) is a strategy they can use to paraphrase and summarize. Paraphrasing involves rewording and reordering the details of a short section of text. Summarizing involves rewording the entire text to explain the main ideas.

3. Model the strategy with students. Quickly read a short passage of text. Think aloud as you pay attention to important information you will later want to take notes on. Model scanning the text to reread and create a list of words and phrases of important

points. Explain to students that they should try not to exceed three words for each point. This will help to avoid plagiarism. This list is the paraphrase.

4. Model creating a short summary paragraph from the list of words and phrases without referring to the original text. This helps to ensure that the important information is captured in the summary and further reduces the possibility of plagiarism.

5. Provide each student with a *Read, Reread, List, Compose* activity sheet. Allow students time to practice RRLC with the remaining texts. Have students share their lists and summaries with partners.

6. Once students are familiar with RRLC, model how to synthesize the individual summaries to one summary about the topic. This helps students understand how they might use RRLC when writing longer reports and essays.

Differentiation

As a scaffold, have students work with partners or in teacher-led small groups to make a list of key words and phrases and compose summaries. Students who demonstrate proficient or advanced skills should use RRLC to evaluate and analyze their paraphrases. They can underline or highlight key words and phrases they used from the text, and evaluate whether they have adhered to guidelines such as borrowing only three words.

Read, Reread, List, Compose *Example*

Read
Read the entire text.

Reread
Scan the text, looking for key information.

List
List important points, no more than three words each.

words can hurt

have deep effects

bullying

repeated verbal abuse

physical abuse

teasing

leaving someone out

spreading rumors

anyone can be victim

bullies lack empathy

have low self-esteem

victim not to blame

bully is to blame

don't ignore bully

speak up

stay calm

tell trusted adult

Compose
Write a summary of the text from the notes on your list.

According to the article "Stop Bullying," bullying is repeated verbal and physical abuse. Bullying can include teasing, leaving someone out, or spreading rumors about them. Even if bullying is just verbal, words can hurt and have deep effects on someone. Anyone can be a victim of bullying, but bullies are often the same. They lack empathy and usually have low self-esteem. It is important to remember that the victim is never to blame for bullying, it is always the bully's fault. If you are a victim of bullying or see bullying, don't ignore it. Stay calm when it happens. Then speak up by finding a trusted adult to tell about the bullying.

Name: _____ Date:_____

Read, Reread, List, Compose

Directions: Read the text. Reread and list key words and phrases. Compose a summary paragraph based on your list.

Read
Read the entire text.

Reread
Scan the text, looking for key information.

List
List important points, no more than three words each.

Compose
Write a summary of the text from the notes on your list.

REFERENCES

Almasi, Janice F., and Susan J. Hart. 2018. "Best Practices in Narrative Text Comprehension Instruction." In *Best Practice in Literacy Instruction*, 6th edition, edited by Lesley Mandel Morrow and Linda B. Gambrell, 221–249. New York: Guilford.

Anderson, Richard Chase, and P. David Pearson. 1984. "A Schema-Theoretic View of Basic Processes in Reading Comprehension." In *Handbook of Reading Research*, edited by P. David Pearson, with Rebecca Barr, Michael L. Kamil, and Peter Mosenthal, 255–291. New York: Routledge.

Armbruster, Bonnie B., Fran Lehr, and Jean Osborn. 2010. *Put Reading First: The Research Building Blocks for Teaching Children to Read: Kindergarten Through Grade 3*. 3rd edition. National Institute for Literacy.

Au, Kathryn H., Jana M. Mason, and Judith A. Scheu. 1995. *Literacy Instruction Today*. Boston: Allyn and Bacon.

Baker, Linda, and Ann L. Brown. 1984. "Metacognitive Skills and Reading." In *Handbook of Reading Research*, edited by P. David. Pearson, Michael L. Kamil, Peter B. Mosenthal, and Rebecca Barr, 353–394. New York: Longman.

Barnes, Douglas, and Frankie Todd. 1995. *Communication and Learning Revisited*. Portsmouth, NH: Heinemann.

Baumann, James F., and Michael F. Graves. 2010. "What Is Academic Vocabulary?" *Journal of Adolescent and Adult Literacy* 54 (1): 4–12. doi.org/10.1598/jaal.54.1.1.

Bear, Donald R., and Diane M. Barone. 1998. *Developing Literacy: An Integrated Approach to Assessment and Instruction*. Boston, MA: Houghton Mifflin.

Bear, Donald R., Marcia Invernizzi, Shane Templeton, and Francine Johnston. 2020. *Words Their Way: Word Study for Phonics, Vocabulary, and Spelling Instruction*. 6th edition. Upper Saddle River, NJ: Pearson.

Beck, Isabel, Margaret G. McKeown, and Linda Kucan. 2002. *Bringing Words to Life: Robust Vocabulary Instruction*. New York: Guilford.

Blachowicz, Camille, and Donna Ogle. 2001. *Reading Comprehension: Strategies for Independent Learners*. New York: Guilford.

Bowers, Peter N., John R. Kirby, and S. Hélène Deacon. 2010. "The Effects of Morphological Instruction on Literacy Skills: A Systematic Review of the Literature." *Review of Educational Research* 80 (2): 144–179. doi.org/10.3102/0034654309359353.

Brozo, William G., and Michele L. Simpson. 2003. *Readers, Teachers, Learners: Expanding Literacy Across the Content Areas*. 4th edition. Upper Saddle River, NJ: Merrill.

Cabell, Sonia Q., and HyeJin Hwang. 2020. "Building Content Knowledge to Boost Comprehension in the Primary Grades." Reading Research Quarterly 55 (S1): S99–S107. doi.org/10.1002/rrq.338.

REFERENCES

Cervetti, Gina N., Tanya S. Wright, and HyeJin Hwang. 2016. "Conceptual Coherence, Comprehension, and Vocabulary Acquisition: A Knowledge Effect?" *Reading and Writing* 29 (4): 761–779. doi.org/10.1007/ 1145-016-9628-x.

Cohen, A. D. 2007. "Coming to Terms with Language Learner Strategies: Surveying the Experts." In *Language Learner Strategies, Volume I,* edited by A. D. Cohen and E. Macaro, 29–45. Oxford: Oxford University Press.

Cromley, Jennifer G., and Roger Azevedo. 2007. "Testing and Refining the Direct and Inferential Mediation Model of Reading Comprehension." *Journal of Educational Psychology* 99 (2): 311–325. doi.org/10.1037/0022-0663.99.2.311.

Cunningham, James W. 1982. "Generating Interactions between Schemata and Text." In *New Inquiries in Reading Research and Instruction,* edited by Jerome A. Niles and Larry A. Harris, 42–47. Rochester, NY: National Reading Conference.

Davis-Haley, Rachel. 2004. "Text What?! What Is Text Rendering?" *Childhood Education* 80 (5): 268-I.

De La Paz, Susan, and Steve Graham. 2002. "Explicitly Teaching Strategies, Skills, and Knowledge: Writing Instruction in Middle School Classrooms." *Journal of Educational Psychology* 94 (4): 687–698. doi.org/10.1037/0022-0663.94.4.687.

De La Paz, Susan, Philip N. Swanson, and Steve Graham. 1998. "Contribution of Executive Control to the Revising Problems of Students with Writing and Learning Difficulties." *Journal of Educational Psychology* 90 (3): 448–460.

Derewianka, Beverly. 2020. *Exploring How Texts Work.* 2nd edition. Newton, NSW: Primary English Teaching Association Australia.

Dewitz, Peter, Michael Graves, Bonnie Graves, and Connie Juel. 2020. *Teaching Reading in the 21st Century: Motivating All Learners.* 6th edition. Saddle River, NJ: Pearson.

Dollins, Cynthia A. 2020. "A Critical Inquiry Approach to Mentor Texts: Learn It With EASE." *The Reading Teacher* 74 (2): 191–199. doi.org/10.1002/trtr.1928.

Dorfman, Lynne R., and Rose Cappelli. 2007. *Mentor Texts: Teaching Writing Through Children's Literature, K-6.* Portland, ME: Stenhouse.

———. 2009. *Nonfiction Mentor Texts: Teaching Informational Writing Through Children's Literature, K-8* (Illustrated). Portland, ME: Stenhouse.

Driscoll, D., and A. Brizee. 2013. "Evaluating Print vs. Internet Sources." The Writing Lab & The OWL at Purdue and Purdue University. owl.english.purdue.edu.

Duke, Nell K., and Kelly B. Cartwright. 2021. "The Science of Reading Progresses: Communicating Advances Beyond the Simple View of Reading." *Reading Research Quarterly* (Special Issue) 56 (S1): S25–S44. doi.org/10.1002/rrq.411.

Duke, Nell K., and P. David Pearson. 2002. "Effective Practices for Developing Reading Comprehension." In *What Research Has to Say About Reading Instruction*, 3rd edition, edited by Alan E. Farstrup and S. Jay Samuels, 205–242. Newark, Delaware: International Reading Association.

Duke, Nell K., Alessandra E. Ward, and P. David Pearson. 2021. "The Science of Reading Comprehension Instruction." *The Reading Teacher* 74 (6): 663–672. doi.org/10.1002/trtr.1993.

Dunlap, Carmen Zuñiga, and Evelyn Marino Weisman. 2006. *Helping English Language Learners Succeed*. Huntington Beach, CA: Shell Education.

Dunn, Patricia A., and Ken Lindblom. 2011. *Grammar Rants: How a Backstage Tour of Writing Complaints Can Help Students Make Informed, Savvy Choices About Their Writing*. Portsmouth, NH: Heinemann.

Durkin, Dolores. 1978. "What Classroom Observations Reveal About Reading Comprehension." *Reading Research Quarterly* 14 (4): 481–553. Newark, Delaware: International Reading Association.

Fisher, Douglas, and Nancy Frey. 2004. *Improving Adolescent Literacy: Content Area Strategies at Work*. Upper Saddle River, NJ: Pearson Education.

———. 2008. *Word Wise and Content Rich, Grades 7-12: Five Essential Steps to Teaching Academic Vocabulary*. Portsmouth, NH: Heinemann.

———. 2012. "Close Reading in Elementary Schools." *The Reading Teacher* 66 (3): 179–188.

———. 2014. "Closely Reading Informational Texts in the Primary Grades." *The Reading Teacher* 68 (3): 222–227. doi.org/10.1002/trtr.1317.

———. 2018. "The Uses and Misuses of Graphic Organizers in Content Area Learning." *The Reading Teacher* 71 (6): 763–766. doi.org/10.1002/trtr.1693.

———. 2020. "No Instructional Minute Wasted: To Avoid Wasting Learning Time, the Best Teachers Do Three Things Differently." *Educational Leadership* 77 (9): 55–60.

Fisher, Douglas, Nancy Frey, and John Almarode. 2022. "Comprehension in Secondary Schools." In *Best Practices in Adolescent Literacy Instruction*, 3rd edition, edited by Kathleen A. Hinchman and Heather K. Sheridan-Thomas, 137–157. New York: Guilford.

Fitzgerald, Jill, and Timothy Shanahan. 2000. "Reading and Writing Relations and Their Development." *Educational Psychologist* 35 (1): 39–50. doi.org/10.1207/5326985ep3501_5.

Fuchs, Lynn S., Douglas Fuchs, Michelle K. Hosp, and Joseph R. Jenkins. 2001. "Oral Reading Fluency as an Indicator of Reading Competence: A Theoretical, Empirical, and Historical Analysis." *Scientific Studies of Reading* 5 (3): 239–256. doi.org/10.1207/532799xssr0503_3.

REFERENCES

Gahn, Shelley Mattson. 1989. "A Practical Guide for Teaching Writing in the Content Areas." *Journal of Reading* 32 (6): 525–531.

Gallagher, Kelly. 2006. *Teaching Adolescent Writers*. Portland, ME: Stenhouse.

Gormley, Kathleen, and Peter McDermott. 2015. "Searching for Evidence—Teaching Students to Become Effective Readers by Visualizing Information in Texts." *The Clearing House: A Journal of Educational Strategies, Issues and Ideas* 88 (6): 171–177.

Gough, Philip B., and William E. Tunmer. 1986. "Decoding, Reading, and Reading Disability." *Remedial and Special Education* 7 (1): 6–10.

Gourgey, Annette F. 1998. "Metacognition in Basic Skills Instruction." *Instructional Science* 26 (1/2): 81–96. Philadelphia: Kluwer Academic Publishers. doi.org/10.1023/a:1003092414893.

Graff, Gerald, and Cathy Birkenstein. 2014. *They Say, I Say: The Moves That Matter in Academic Writing*. 3rd edition. New York: Norton.

Graham, Steve. 2020. "The Sciences of Reading and Writing Must Become More Fully Integrated." *Reading Research Quarterly* 55 (S1): S35–S44. doi.org/10.1002/rrq.332.

Graham, Steve, Alisha Bollinger, Carol Booth Olson, Catherine D'Aoust, Charles MacArthur, Deborah McCutchen, Natalie and Olinghouse. 2012a. *Teaching Elementary School Students to Be Effective Writers: A Practice Guide* (NCEE 20124058). Washington, DC: National Center for Education Evaluation and Regional Assistance, Institute of Education Sciences, U.S. Department of Education. Retrieved from the NCEE website: http://whatworks.ed.gov.

Graham, Steve, Julie Bruch, Jill Fitzgerald, Linda D. Friedrich, Joshua Furgeson, Katie Greene, James Kim, Julia Lyskawa, Carol Booth Olson, and Claire Smither Wulsin. 2017. *Teaching Secondary Students to Write Effectively: A Practice Guide*. Washington, DC: National Center for Education Evaluation and Regional Assistance (NCEE), Institute of Education Sciences, U.S. Department of Education. Retrieved from the NCEE website: http://whatworks.ed.gov.

Graham, Steve, and Michael Hebert. 2010. *Writing to Read: Evidence for How Writing Can Improve*. A Carnegie Corporation Time to Act Report. Washington, DC: Alliance for Excellent Education.

Graham, Steve, Debra McKeown, Sharlene Kiuhara, and Karen R. Harris. 2012b. "A Meta-Analysis of Writing Instruction for Students in the Elementary Grades." *Journal of Educational Psychology* 104 (4): 879–896. doi.org/10.1037/a0029185.

Graham, Steve, and Dolores Perin. 2007. "A Meta-Analysis of Writing Instruction for Adolescent Students." *Journal of Educational Psychology* 99 (3): 445–476. doi.org/10.1037/0022-0663.99.3.445.

Hacker, Douglas J., John Dunlosky, and Arthur C. Graesser. 1998. *Metacognition in Educational Theory and Practice*. Mahwah, New Jersey: L. Erlbaum Associates.

Halliday, M. A. K. 1975. *Learning How to Mean: Explorations in the Development of Language.* London: Edward Arnold.

Harris, Karen R., Steve Graham, Linda H. Mason, and Barbara Friedlander. 2008. *Powerful Writing Strategies for all Students.* Baltimore, MD: Brookes.

Harvey, Stephanie, and Anne Goudvis. 2017. *Strategies That Work: Teaching Comprehension for Engagement, Understanding, and Building Knowledge, Grades K–8.* 3rd edition. Portland, ME: Stenhouse.

Hattie, John. 2009. *Visible Learning: A Synthesis of Over 800 Meta-Analyses Relating to Achievement.* New York: Routledge.

Hayes, David A. 1989. "Helping Students GRASP the Knack of Writing Summaries." *Journal of Reading* 33 (2): 96–101.

Hochman, Judith C., and Natalie Wexler. 2017. "One Sentence at a Time: The Need for Explicit Instruction in Teaching Students to Write Well." *American Educator*, Summer 2017. American Federation of Teachers. aft.org/ae/summer2017/hochman-wexler.

Hollie, Sharroky. 2018. *Culturally and Linguistically Responsive Teaching and Learning, Second Edition.* Huntington Beach, CA: Shell Education.

Hoover, Wesley A., and Philip B. Gough. 1990. "The Simple View of Reading." *Reading and Writing: An Interdisciplinary Journal* 2 (2): 127–160. doi.org/10.1007/BF00401799.

Hoover, Wesley A., and William E. Tunmer. 2018. "The Simple View of Reading: Three Assessments of Its Adequacy." *Remedial and Special Education* 39 (5): 304–312. Crossref, doi.org/10.1177/0741932518773154.

———. 2020. *The Cognitive Foundations of Reading and Its Acquisition: A Framework with Applications Connecting Teaching and Learning (Literacy Studies).* London: Springer.

———. 2022. "The Primacy of Science in Communicating Advances in the Science of Reading." *Reading Research Quarterly* (57) 2: 399–408. doi.org/10.1002/rrq.446.

Hulit, Lloyd M., Merle R. Howard, and Kathleen R. Fahey. 2018. *Born to Talk: An Introduction to Speech and Language Development.* 7th edition. Boston: Allyn and Bacon.

Jouhar, Mohammed R., and William H. Rupley. 2020. "The Reading-Writing Connection based on Independent Reading and Writing: A Systematic Review." *Reading and Writing Quarterly* 37 (2): 136–156. doi.org/10.1080/10573569.2020.1740632.

Jump, Jennifer, and Robin D. Johnson. 2023. *What the Science of Reading Says about Word Recognition.* Huntington Beach, CA: Shell Education.

Jump, Jennifer, and Kathleen Kopp. 2023. *What the Science of Reading Says about Reading Comprehension and Content Knowledge.* Huntington Beach, CA: Shell Education.

Jump, Jennifer, and Hillary Wolfe. 2023. *What the Science of Reading Says about Writing.* Huntington Beach, CA: Shell Education.

REFERENCES

Kamil, Michael L., Geoffrey D. Borman, Janice Dole, Cathleen C. Kral, Terry Salinger, and Joseph Torgesen. 2008. *Improving Adolescent Literacy: Effective Classroom and Intervention Practices: A Practice Guide* (NCEE #2008-4027). Washington, DC: National Center for Education Evaluation and Regional Assistance, Institute of Education Sciences, U.S. Department of Education.

Kettel, Raymond P., and Danielle L. DeFauw. 2018. "Paraphrase Without Plagiarism: Use RRLC (Read, Reread, List, Compose)." *The Reading Teacher* 72 (2): 245–255.

Kiuhara, Sharlene A., Robert E. O'Neill, Leanne S. Hawken, and Steve Graham. 2012. "The Effectiveness of Teaching 10th Grade Students STOP, AIMS, and DARE for Planning and Drafting Persuasive Text." *Exceptional Children* 78 (3): 335–355.

Koster, Monica, Elena Tribushinina, Peter De Jong, and H. H. Van den Bergh. 2015. "Teaching Children to Write: A Meta-Analysis of Writing Intervention Research." *Journal of Writing Research* 7 (2): 249–274. doi.org/10.17239/jowr-2015.07.02.2.

Kozen, Alice A., Rosemary K. Murray, and Idajean Windell. 2006. "Increasing All Students' Chance to Achieve." *Intervention in School and Clinic* 41 (4): 195–200. doi.org/10.1177/10534512060410040101

Krashen, Stephen. 2009. "81 Generalizations about Free Voluntary Reading." IATEFL Young Learner and Teenager Special Interest Group Publication. successfulenglish.com/wp-content/uploads/2010/01/81-Generalizations-about-FVR-2009.pdf.

Lee, Carol D., and Anika Spratley. 2010. "Reading in the Disciplines: The Challenges of Adolescent Literacy." Final Report. Carnegie Corporation of New York's Council on Advancing Adolescent Literacy.

Lemov, Doug, Colleen Driggs, and Erica Woolway. 2016. *Reading Reconsidered: A Practical Guide to Rigorous Literacy Instruction*. San Francisco: Jossey-Bass.

Lenz, B. Keith, and Charles A. Hughes. 1990. "A Word Identification Strategy for Adolescents with Learning Disabilities." *Journal of Learning Disabilities* 23 (3): 149–158. doi.org/10.1177/002221949002300304

LeVasseur, Valerie Marciarille, Paul Macaruso, and Donald Shankweiler. 2008. "Promoting Gains in Reading Fluency: A Comparison of Three Approaches." *Reading and Writing* 21 (3): 205–230. doi.org/10.1007/ 1145-007-9070-1.

McCrostie, James. 2007. Examining Learner Vocabulary Notebooks. *ELT Journal* 61 (3): 246–255. doi.org/10.1093/elt/ccm032.

Middle School Matters Institute. 2023. "Get the GIST Log for Students." *Get the Gist (Main Idea) Toolkit*. greatmiddleschools.org/toolkits/reading/get-the-gist/.

Moats, Louisa C. 2020. "Teaching Reading Is Rocket Science." *American Educator*, Summer 2020. aft.org/ae/summer2020/moats.

Moore, David W., and Sharon Arthur Moore, Patricia M. Cunningham, and James W. Cunningham. 2002. *Developing Readers and Writers in the Content Areas K–12.* 5th ed. Boston: Allyn and Bacon.

Morrow, Lesley Mandel. 2003. "Motivating Lifelong Voluntary Readers." In *Handbook of Research on Teaching the English Language Arts*, edited by James Flood, Diane Lapp, James R. Squire, and Julie M. Jenson, 857–867. Mahwah, NJ: Lawrence Erlbaum Associates.

National Early Literacy Panel. 2008. *Developing Early Literacy: Report of the National Early Literacy Panel: A Scientific Synthesis of Early Literacy Development and Implications for Intervention.* Jessup, MD: National Institute for Literacy with National Center for Family Literacy.

National Reading Panel (U.S.) and National Institute of Child Health and Human Development (U.S.). 2000. *Report of the National Reading Panel: Teaching Children to Read: An Evidence-based Assessment of the Scientific Research Literature on Reading and Its Implications for Reading Instruction.* Bethesda: U.S. Dept. of Health and Human Services, Public Health Service, National Institutes of Health, National Institute of Child Health and Human Development.

Paige, David D. 2011. "16 Minutes of 'Eyes-on-Text' Can Make a Difference: Whole-Class Choral Reading as an Adolescent Fluency Strategy." *Reading Horizons* 51 (1): 1–20.

Paige, David D., and Theresa Magpuri-Lavell. 2014. "Reading Fluency in the Middle and Secondary Grades." *International Electronic Journal of Elementary Education* 7 (1): 83–96.

Paige, David D., Timothy Rasinski, Theresa Magpuri-Lavell, Grant S. Smith. 2014. "Interpreting the Relationships Among Prosody, Automaticity, Accuracy, and Silent Reading Comprehension in Secondary Students." *Journal of Literacy Research* 46 (2): 123–56. doi.org/10.1177/1086296x14535170.

Palinscar, Annemarie Sullivan, and Ann L. Brown. 1984. "Reciprocal Teaching of Comprehension-Fostering and Comprehension-Monitoring Activities." *Cognition and Instruction* 1 (2): 117–175. doi.org/10.1207/ 532690xci0102_1.

Paris, Scott G., Marjorie Y. Lipson, and Karen K. Wixson. 1983. "Becoming a Strategic Reader." *Contemporary Educational Psychology* 8 (3): 293–316. doi.org/10.1016/0361-476x(83)90018-8.

Perfetti, Charles A. 1995. "Cognitive Research Can Inform Reading Education." *Journal of Research in Reading* 18 (2): 106-115.

———. 1998. "Two Basic Questions about Reading and Learning to Read." In *Problems and Interventions in Literacy Development*, edited by Pieter Reitsma and Ludo Verhoeven, 15–48. Dordrecht, The Netherlands: Kluwer Academic Publishers.

REFERENCES

Perfetti, Charles A., Ying Liu, Julie Fiez, Jessica Nelson, Donald J. Bolger, and Li-Hai Tan. 2007. "Reading in Two Writing Systems: Accommodation and Assimilation of the Brain's Reading Network." *Bilingualism: Language and Cognition* 10 (2): 131–46. doi.org/10.1017/ 366728907002891.

Perfetti, Charles, and Joseph Stafura. 2013. "Word Knowledge in a Theory of Reading Comprehension." *Scientific Studies of Reading* 18 (1): 22–37. doi.org/10.1080/10888438.2 013.827687.

Pressley, Michael, and Peter Afflerbach. 1995. *Verbal Protocols of Reading: The Nature of Constructively Responsive Reading.* New York: Routledge.

Pressley, Michael, John G. Borkowski, and Wolfgang Schneider. 1987. "Cognitive Strategies: Good Strategy Users Coordinate Metacognition and Knowledge." *Annals of Child Development* 4: 89–129.

Pressley, Michael, Sara E. Dolezal, Lisa M. Raphael, Lindsey Mohan, Alysia D. Roehrig, and Kristen Bogner. 2003. *Motivating Primary-Grade Students.* New York: Guilford.

Rafdal, Brooke H., Kristen L. McMaster, Scott R. McConnell, Douglas Fuchs, and Lynn S. Fuchs. 2011. "The Effectiveness of Kindergarten Peer-Assisted Learning Strategies for Students with Disabilities." *Exceptional Children* 77 (3): 299–316. doi. org/10.1177/001440291107700303.

RAND. 2003. "Developing an R&D Program to Improve Reading Comprehension." *RAND Research Brief.* doi.org/10.7249/rb8024.

Rasinski, Timothy V., and Nancy Padak. 2005. "Fluency beyond the Primary Grades: Helping Adolescent Struggling Readers." *Voices From the Middle* 13 (1): 34–41.

Rasinski, Timothy, David Paige, Cameron Rains, Fran Stewart, Brenda Julovich, Deb Prenkert, William H. Rupley, and William Dee Nichols. 2017. "Effects of Intensive Fluency Instruction on the Reading Proficiency of Third-Grade Struggling Readers." *Reading and Writing Quarterly* 33 (6): 519–532. doi.org/10.1080/10573569.2016 .1250144.

Rayner, Keith, Alexander Pollatsek, Jane Ashby, and Charles Clifton Jr. 2012. *Psychology of Reading.* 2nd edition. New York: Psychology Press

Rupley, William H., John W. Logan, and William D. Nichols. 1999. "Vocabulary Instruction in a Balanced Reading Program." *The Reading Teacher* 52 (4): 336–346. Newark, Delaware: International Reading Association.

Ryder, Randall J., and Michael F. Graves. 2003. *Reading and Learning in Content Areas.* 3rd edition. Hoboken, NJ: John Wiley and Sons.

Santa, Carol M., Lynn T. Havens, and Bonnie J. Valdes. 1995. *Project CRISS (Creating Independence Through Student-Owned Strategies.* 3rd edition. Dubuque, IA: Kendall/Hunt.

Scarborough, Hollis S. 2001. "Connecting Early Language and Literacy to Later Reading (Dis)abilities: Evidence, Theory, and Practice." In *Handbook of Early Literacy Research*, edited by Susan B. Neuman and David K. Dickinson, 97–110. New York: Guilford.

Sedita, Joan. 2019. "The Strands That Are Woven into Skilled Writing." keystoliteracy.com/wp-content/uploads/2020/02/The-Strands-That-Are-Woven-Into-Skilled-WritingV2.pdf

Sinatra, Richard, Vicky Zygouris-Coe, and Sheryl B. Dasinger. 2012. "Preventing a Vocabulary Lag: What Lessons Are Learned from Research." *Reading and Writing Quarterly* 28 (4): 333–357. doi.org/10.1080/10573569.2012.702040.

Singer, Bonnie D., and Anthony S. Bashir. 2004. "EmPOWER: A Strategy for Teaching Students with Language Learning Disabilities How to Write Expository Text." In *Language and Literacy Learning in Schools*, edited by Elaine R. Silliman and Louise Wilkinson, 239–72. New York: Guilford.

Snow, Catherine E. 2018. "Simple and Not-So-Simple Views of Reading." *Remedial and Special Education* 39 (5) 313–316. doi.org/10.1177/0741932518770288.

Stengel-Eskin, Elias, Tzu-ray Su, Matt Post, and Benjamin Van Durme. 2019. "A Discriminative Neural Model for Cross-Lingual Word Alignment." *Proceedings of the 2019 Conference on Empirical Methods in Natural Language Processing and the 9th International Joint Conference on Natural Language Processing (EMNLP-IJCNLP)*. doi.org/10.18653/v1/d19-1084.

Sticht, Thomas G., and James H. James. 1984. "Listening and Reading." In *Handbook of Reading Research*, edited by P. David Pearson, with Rebecca Barr, Michael L. Kamil, and Peter Mosenthal, 293–318. New York: Routledge.

Swanson, Elizabeth, Sharon Vaughn, and Jade Wexler. 2017. "Enhancing Adolescents' Comprehension of Text by Building Vocabulary Knowledge." *TEACHING Exceptional Children* 50 (2): 84–94. doi.org/10.1177/0040059917720777.

Taba, Hilda. 1967. *Teacher's Handbook for Elementary Social Studies*. Reading, Massachusetts: Addison-Wesley.

Templeton, Shane, Donald Bear, Marcia Invernizzi, Francine Johnston, Kevin Flanigan, Dianna Townsend, Lori Helman, and Latisha Hayes. 2015. *Words Their Way: Vocabulary for Middle and Secondary Students,* 2nd edition. Boston: Pearson.

Tileston, Donna Walker. 2006. *Teaching Strategies for Active Learning: Five Essentials for Your Teaching Plan*. Thousand Oaks, CA: Corwin.

Tomlinson, Carol A. 2014. *The Differentiated Classroom: Responding to the Needs of All Learners*. 2nd edition. Alexandria, VA: ASCD.

Tompkins, Gail. 2001. *Language Arts: Content and Teaching Strategies*. 5th edition. Saddle River, NJ: Pearson.

REFERENCES

Tompkins, Gail. 2018. *Teaching Writing: Balancing Process and Product*. 7th edition. Saddle River, NJ: Pearson.

Topping, K., A. Thurston, K. McGavock, and N. Conlin. 2012. "Outcomes and Process in Reading Tutoring." *Educational Research* 54 (3): 239–258. doi.org/10.1080/00131881.2012.710086

Walters, JoDee, and Neval Bozkurt. 2009. "The Effect of Keeping Vocabulary Notebooks on Vocabulary Acquisition." *Language Teaching Research* 13 (4): 403–423. doi.org/10.1177/1362168809341509

Wattenberg, Ruth. 2016. "Inside the Common Core Reading Tests: Why the Best Prep Is a Knowledge-Rich Curriculum." *Knowledge Matters*, Issue Brief #7, knowledgematterscampaign.org/wp-content/uploads/2016/09/Wattenberg.pdf.

Watts-Taffe, Susan, Carolyn B. Gwinn, and Chris Forrest. 2018. "Explain, Engage, Extend, Examine: Four E's of Vocabulary Instruction." *Texas Journal of Literacy Education* 7 (1): 25–43.

Willingham, Daniel T. 2006. "How Knowledge Helps: It Speeds and Strengthens Reading Comprehension, Learning—and Thinking." *American Educator*, Spring 2006. American Federation of Teachers. aft.org/periodical/american-educator/spring-2006/how-knowledge-helps.

Digital Resources

Accessing the Digital Resources

The digital resources can be downloaded by following these steps:

1. Go to www.tcmpub.com/digital
2. Use the 13-digit ISBN number to redeem the digital resources.
3. Respond to the question using the book.
4. Follow the prompts on the Content Cloud website to sign in or create a new account.
5. The content redeemed will appear on your My Content screen. Click on the product to look through the digital resources. All file resources are available for download. Select files can be previewed, opened, and shared. Any web-based content, such as videos, links, or interactive text, can be viewed and used in the browser but is not available for download.

For questions and assistance please contact Teacher Created Materials.

email: customerservice@tcmpub.com

phone: 800-858-7339

Contents of the Digital Resources

The digital resources include templates for the student activity pages in this book.

www.ingramcontent.com/pod-product-compliance
Lightning Source LLC
Chambersburg PA
CBHW060421010526
44118CB00017B/2309